African Indians

Timely Entrance, Expansion and Settlement

Author

SAMPSON JEREMIAH

SONITTEC PUBLISHING. All rights reserved. No part of this publication may be reproduced, distributed, or transmitted in any form or by any means, including photocopying, recording, or other electronic or mechanical methods, without the prior written permission of the publisher, except in the case of brief quotations embodied in critical reviews and certain other noncommercial uses permitted by copyright law. For permission requests, write to the publisher, addressed "Attention: Permissions Coordinator," at the address below.

Copyright © 2019 Sonittec Publishing
All Rights Reserved

First Printed: 2019.

Publisher:
SONITTEC LTD
College House, 2nd Floor
17 King Edwards Road,
Ruislip
London
HA4 7AE.

Table of Content

Outline 1
Early Indians in African 2
   Roots: 2
   Language, Tradition and beliefs: 5
   The Wragg Commission of (1885 - 1887) 7
      A short-term of the Wragg Commission: 8
1947-Joint Declaration of Collaboration 13
   The ANC, APO and the Indian Congresses debate teamwork 16
   Africans look Eastward -- Professor Jabavu 18
   Non-European Conference Plans of NIC 19
A face of fight 22
Indian Regulation Struggle 34
Gandhi and the Passive Struggle Campaign 1907-1914 39
   Mohandas Karamchand Gandhi 43
      Early life and education 43
      Gandhi in South Africa 44
      Satyagraha 54
      Return to India 62
      The title 'Mahatma' 63
   Satyagraha: the first campaign 65
   The First Campaign 67
   Between the two campaigns 72
   The 1913 Campaign: Strikers and Marchers 74
   The Compromise 79
   The Aftermath in South Africa 80
   International Legacy 81
The Last of The Gandhians in South Africa 84
Indenture: A new system of slavery? 96
Community of Indians 128
   Indian passive resistance in South Africa: 1946 – 1948 128
   Passenger Indians 129
   Areas of Settlement 131
   Education 135
   Unemployment and poverty 137
   Family, religion and language 137
   Religion 139
   Mosques and Temples 139
   Religious education and drama 143
   Festivals 145

- *Kavadi* *147*
- *Mariamman* *148*
- *Draupadi (firewalking)* *148*
- *Diwali* *149*
- *Language* *149*
- *Cuisine* *151*
- *Social Customs* *152*

Community of Indian in Lenasia **154**

Indian education in Natal **197**

Mandela: Message to India **215**

Indian People of South History in more detail **219**
- *The Indian struggle for civil rights before 1948:* *226*
- *Political involvement after 1948:* *228*
- *Indian South Africans today – the fast facts:* *232*
- *The Legacy of the Indian South Africans:* *233*

Indian Opinion' newspaper **237**
- *History of the 'Indian Opinion' newspaper* *237*

End of the Book **248**

Outline

This book is about Indians in South Africa, the early migration of Indians to South Africa, their pre-occupation, involving in South African Affairs and Politics and other aspect of Indians in their South African home. Education, Religion and the Indian community will also be detailed in this book

Is about nearly one million Indians living in South Africa, 80 per cent reside in KwaZulu-Natal. But Indians are not a culturally homogeneous group and have no distinct language and religious differences between them although English is widely spoken by most Indians. The Indians in KwaZulu-Natal are predominantly Hindu while those living in and around Cape Town are mainly Muslim. About 5 per cent of Indians are Christians.

Sampson Jeremiah

Early Indians in African

From bondage to freedom - The 150th anniversary of the arrival of Indian workers in South Africa

The feature on Indian South Africans forms part of our larger feature on the People of South Africa. It is a long term project to build a comprehensive overview of the rich diversity of peoples, traditions and culture that address the question, 'Who are South Africans?' This year, 2010, is the 150th anniversary of the arrival of the Indian indentured labourers and the birth of this community in South Africa. We are using this to launch and major project to build a comprehensive social and political history of this African community.

Roots:

South Africans of Indian origin comprise a heterogeneous community distinguished by different origins, languages, and religious beliefs. The first Indians arrived during the Dutch colonial era, as slaves, in 1684. A conservative calculation based strictly on records shows over 16 300 slaves from the Indian subcontinent having been brought to the Cape. In the decades 1690 to 1725 over 80% of the slaves were Indians. This practice continued until the end of slavery in 1838. They made up the majority of slaves that came from the Far East and were by the 1880s totally integrated into the Cape White and Coloured communities.

In the second half if the 19th Century, Indians came to South Africa in two categories, namely as indentured workers in 1860 and later as 'free' or 'passenger' Indians. The former came as a result of a triangular pact among three governments, which stated that the indentured Indians were to work for the Natal colonial government on Natal's sugar plantations. The 'free' Indians came to South Africa mainly as traders alert to new opportunities abroad. These 'free Indians' came at their own expense from India, Mauritius, and other places. However, emigration was stopped in 1914.

Between November 1860 and 1911(when the system of indentured labour was stopped) nearly 152 184 indentured labourers from across India arrived in Natal. After serving their indentures, the first category of Indians were free to remain in South Africa or to return to India. By 1910, nearly 26.85% indentured men returned to India, but most chose to stay and thus constituted the forbearers of the majority of present-day South African Indians.

With 1994 and the advent of a democratic constitution, immigration policy restrictions, imposed by the apartheid regime, were scrapped. People from India, Pakistan, Sri Lanka and Bangladesh, arrived in South Africa as new immigrants. However, there is a major cultural division between these new groups and Indian South Africans.

A key factor that helped forge a common South African "Indian" identity was the political struggles waged against harsh discriminatory laws enacted against Indians and the other Black oppressed groups in the country. As a consequence, the Indian community established a number of political formations, the most prominent being the Natal Indian Congress (NIC) established by Gandhi in 1894, and the Transvaal and Cape Indian Congresses in the early part of the 20th century. Members of the Indian Congress, together with socialist activists in the Communist Party of South Africa were instrumental, from the 1930s, in building cross racial alliances. The small Indian, Coloured and White progressive sectors joined with progressive African activists and together, they conducted a common non-racial struggle for Freedom and Equality.

Language, Tradition and beliefs:

English is spoken as a first language by most Indian South Africans, although a minority of the Indian South African population, especially the elders, still speak some Indian languages. These languages include Hindi, Tamil, Telugu, Urdu, Punjabi, and Gujarati. Indian South Africans are predominantly Hindu, but Muslims, Christians, and Sikhs also came to South Africa from India from as early as 1860.

Hindu, the most prominent religion in India, originated 5000 years ago. The Hindu religion prescribes a three fold approach to serving God. This approach includes knowledge, or the studying of the Bhagavad-Gita and other texts; yoga, to connect both body and mind, and devotion or *bhakti*, which promotes serving God through prayer and benevolent acts. Notable Hindu festivals include Diwali/Deepavali, the festival of lights, and the Tamil Thai Poosam Kavady annual festival.

Muslim/Islamic influence began in South Africa with the arrival of indentured workers from the west and south coast of India. As only 7-10% of these workers were Muslim, Sheikh Ahmad, the founding father of Islam in Natal, and later Soofie Saheb ensured that impoverished Muslim Indians were not drawn to Hinduism. Therefore, a concerted effort was made to retain their religious heritage, through the demarcation of Islamic festivals and the establishment of Muslim schools or *madrasahs*.

The Islamic community continues to thrive in South Africa, in both Natal and the Western Cape - where indentured labourers moved with their families after the completion of their contracts. Followers of the Muslim faith are committed to praying at least five times a day, and are not permitted to drink alcohol. Notable Muslim celebrations include Eid, and Ramadan.

The Sikh faith forms a slender portion of the local population, and is a religion influenced by both Hindu and Islam. The Sikh religion is concerned with a belief in *One Immortal Being* and ten gurus. Many Sikhs wear an iron or steel bracelet as a symbol of their devotion to their religion. Originating in the Punjab region, prominent Sikh celebrations include Parkash Utsav, which celebrates '*Divine Light*' or '*Divine Knowledge*'.

The diverse Indian population in South Africa is concentrated in Kwa-Zulu Natal's largest city, Durban, which has the most substantial Indian population in sub-Saharan Africa. South Africa as a whole also has a substantial Indian population, with over 1 million people of Indian descent. Therefore, Indian influences have contributed to the multi-cultural diversity of South Africa. The local culinary landscape has been infused with a diverse array of Oriental flavour - most notably in the Natal region. Popular dishes include curry, and an intrinsic Durban dish called 'bunny chow', which is half a loaf of bread, hollowed out and filled with curry.

South African Indians retain a sense of cultural and social connection to India, and a concept of primary local and secondary ancestral identity is prevalent among people of Indian descent.

The Wragg Commission of (1885 - 1887)

Indian immigration into Natal brought with it strained relations and severe problems and conflicts between the White colonists and the new arrivals. Within a decade, irregularities in the employment of Indians had increased to such an extent that that the Natal Colonial Secretary was forced to set up a special Indian Immigrants Commission in 1885, to investigate the conditions and complaints of Indian immigrants.

The Governor, Sir Henry Ernest Bulwer appointed the Wragg Commission as it came to be known consisted of Mr Justice Walter Thomas Wragg, James Renault Saunders, J.P. Dr Robert Lewer, Senior Medical Officer and Henry Francis Richardson.

The Commission's Report was a document of the prevailing legislation in the Colony of Natal governing Indian immigrants. According to the author, CG Henning, the lengthy report of the Wragg Commission presents a rather haphazard method of collecting and presenting facts. Many witnesses were called several times and the interrogation does not follow any pattern of logic.

A short-term of the Wragg Commission:

- Medical: The smoking of dagga was considered illegal as it led to crime and absenteeism from work. Bilharzia was common in certain areas and leprosy occurred in a small minority. Veneral diseases were a serious problem especially amongst single women. It was recommended that stricter checks be made at Calcutta and Madras as well as on disembarkation at Durban. There was an increase in the consumption of liquor. The Durban Depot Hospital was found to be totally unsatisfactory in the treatment of the sick. The hospital was understaffed and there was no female nurse here. Male and female patients were not separated. The toilet facilities were very primitive while the supply of drugs was inadequate. The Report went on to state that greater attention should be given to special diets for patients.

> Social Aspects: by 1885 the Indian population had reached around 30 000. Between 1873 and 30 June 1886, 4 971 Indian marriages were registered, of which 865 were still under indenture. By 1885 there were eight divorces in Natal. According to the commission, it was lawful for an Indian boy of 16 and an Indian girl of 13 to marry. The Durban cemetery was regarded as a "disgrace and dangerous to health". Pigs (belonging to a nearby butcher) "trespassed and rooted up the bodies of the dead". The Commission recommended that the indiscriminate burying of the dead should cease and that Indian graveyards "be maintained with decency and due respect for the dead".

The Commission condemned the Railway Barracks at Durban, the barracks at the Central Station and at the Point for their faulty construction. It was recommended that the Medical Officer regularly inspect huts on the estates for cleanliness and sanitary arrangements. Water supply for consumption on most Estates was fouled by pollution and was of grave concern. Rivers and streams were used for personal ablution and the washing of clothes, but also to obey the call of nature. Estate owners were to sink wells that were well protected and that latrines were to be constructed on the estates for usage. Municipal by-laws prohibited the construction of thatched buildings and in rural areas these were also considered illegal as it was a hazard in the event of grass fires. There was a rise in drunkenness in Natal.

- Pollution: many Indians suffered from bilharzias as a result of bathing in streams and drawing water from here. Also latrines were not provided by estate owners. As a result the Chief Medical Officer also played the role of the Sanitary Inspector.

- Labour: shockingly, the Commission emphasised only two cases of ill-treatment of Indians. Sundays, Good Friday, Christmas Day and New Years Day were regarded as days of rest. The Commission partially agreed to a request for Sunday working, namely, feeding animals etc., and those employees should work for two hours on Sunday before 8a.m. The Commission was vague on the status of women who did not work, leaving the door open to irregularities and abuse.

- The Protector's Office: the Commission was extremely critical of the position of the Protector and recommended that some of his judicial powers be repealed. It further recommended that the Protectors courts be abolished and that all cases be heard by the Resident Magistrate.

> The Wragg Commission reported that, " - - - Free Indians thrive in Natal. Their wants are, comparatively, few, and their industrious habits cause them to prosper in nearly every occupation in which they engage". In market gardening they soon supplanted all other rivals and took over the industry. Street hawkers maintained a door-to-door fresh vegetable service in Durban. Through the coastal belt of Natal they cleared land for cultivating sugar, maize, tobacco or vegetables. As domestic servants many earned £4 per month and even more as cooks.

On Salisbury Island, in Durban Bay, there was a thriving fish industry with their dried salt fish finding its ways to markers in Pietermaritzburg, Ladysmith and even as far as Mauritius. It is interesting to note the comments of one Sir Henry Binns, appearing before the Commission, " - - - Free Indians have grown about 100 000 muids of maize per annum. We have never had any immigrants from Europe who have shown any inclination to become market gardeners and fishermen".

> Some Colonists felt that Indians should remain indentured for ten years or, alternatively, they should be sent back to India after five years unless they were willing to re-indenture for a further period. The "free" Indians status should be reduced and that he

should carry identity documents and that their freedom of movement and place of residence or business should be restricted. Another group of Colonists demanded that all Indian labour should cease and that Blacks should be employed.

After three years of intensive research gathering evidence from witnesses, the Commission compiled an elaborate report. The Commission seemed to have failed to reach a satisfactory solution to the "problem" of Indian immigration.

1947-Joint Declaration of Collaboration

1947

"Joint Declaration of Cooperation" Signed by Dr A.B. Xuma, President of the African National Congress, Dr G.M. Naicker, President of the Natal Indian Congress and Dr Y.M. Dadoo, President of the Transvaal Indian Congress ("Three Doctors' Pact"), 9 March 1947

This Joint Meeting between the representatives of the African National Congress and the Natal and Transvaal Indian Congresses, having fully realised the urgency of cooperation between the non-European peoples and other democratic forces for the attainment of basic human rights and full citizenship for all sections of the South African people, has resolved that a Joint Declaration of Cooperation is imperative for the working out of a practical basis of cooperation between the national organisations of the non-European peoples.

This Joint Meeting declares its sincerest conviction that to his the future progress, goodwill, good race relations, and for the building of a united, greater and free South Africa, full franchise rights must be extended to all sections of the South African people, and to his end this Joint Meeting pledges the fullest cooperation between the African and Indian peoples and appeals to all democratic and freedom loving citizens of South Africa to support fully and cooperate in this struggle for:

1. Full franchise.

2. Equal economic and industrial rights and opportunities and the recognition of African trade unions under the Industrial Conciliation Act.

3. The removal of all land restrictions against non-European and the provision of adequate housing facilities for all non-Europeans.

4. The extension of free and compulsory education to non-European

5. Guaranteeing freedom of movement and the abolition of Pass Laws against the African people and the provincial barriers against Indians.

6. And the removal of all discriminatory and oppressive legislation from the Union's statute book.

This Joint Meeting is therefore of the opinion that for the attainment of these objects it is urgently necessary that a vigorous campaign be immediately launched and that every effort be made to compel the Union government to implement the United Nations decisions and to treat the non-European peoples in South Africa in conformity with the principles of the United Nations Charter.

This Joint Meeting further resolves to meet from time to time 'implement this Declaration and to take active steps in proceeding with the campaign.

ANC, TIC and NIC call for Full Franchise

Johannesburg, Sunday: At a joint meeting of the representatives of the African National Congress, the Natal Indian Congress and the Transvaal Indian Congress, held here today, a resolution was passed calling for full franchise, equal economic and industrial rights, the removal of non-European land restrictions, free and compulsory Nation, freedom of movement and the abolition of the pass laws. The statement is signed by Dr A. B. Xuma, the President-General of the African National Congress, Dr G.M. Naicker, the President of the Natal Indian Congress, and Dr Y.M. Dadoo, President of the Transvaal Indian Congress. The following is the text of the resolution:

"This joint meeting between the representatives of the African National Congress and the Natal and Transvaal Indian Congresses, having fully realised the urgency of cooperation between the non-European peoples and other democratic forces for the attainment of basis human rights and full citizenship for all sections of the South African people, has resolved that a joint declaration of cooperation is imperative for the working out of a practical basis of cooperation between the national organisations of the non-European peoples."

"This joint meeting declares its sincerest conviction that for the future progress, goodwill, good race relations and for the building of a united, greater and free South Africa, full franchise rights must be extend to all sections of the South African people, and to this end this joint meeting pledges the fullest cooperation between the African and Indian peoples and appeals to all democratic and freedom-loving citizens of South Africa, to support fully and cooperate in this struggle for full franchise."

The ANC, APO and the Indian Congresses debate teamwork

Mr. M.D. Naidoo, on his return from Johannesburg, where he attended, on behalf of the Natal Indian Congress, the meeting oil-March between the African National Congress, the APO and the Natal and Transvaal Indian Congresses, stated that "the desire to evolve some method whereby the distinctive efforts of the different non-European communities to bring to an end colour discrimination may be coordinated and of assistance to each other was as keenly expressed by the African and coloured delegates as by the Indian delegates.

"The decision to hold meetings under the joint auspices of the three national organisations in Johannesburg and Durban is the first step in translating into reality the historic declaration issued on 9 March. The persistent attempt of reactionary European groups to sow discord and widen the breach has failed. On the other hand, the gulf has been bridged and a sure foundation laid on which the structure of permanent cooperation may be built.

It should be emphasised once again that the recognition of a common basic pattern in me laws applying to the different races in South Africa which has led links being forged between the African National Congress, the APU and the Indian Congresses does not mean that an anti-White movement is being launched. The non-European people are joining hands because it is as non-Europeans that they are deprived of democratic rights and subjected to racially oppressive laws.

They would welcome the friendship and assistance of democratic Europeans. It requires to be emphasised also that this coordination does not mean a submergence of identity or a loss of independence. On the contrary, it should be a source of strength that the efforts of one should assist the other and thereby make cooperation more fruitful. It may now be said that the winning of democratic rights has been brought appreciably nearer.

Africans look Eastward -- Professor Jabavu

"A link-up based on affinity of colour will be next move in consolidating the position of the non-European in South Africa. Denied human rights in this country, Africans will look to the east, particularly India, which is now on the eve of attaining sovereign status, as the champion of the coloured races of the world," said Professor D.D.T. Jabavu, who is now in Maritzburg, in the course of an interview to a Leader representative.

"I fear that unless something is done quickly to disabuse the minds of Africans concerning their white rulers' policy, there will develop a significant trend towards separation of whites and blacks sentiment -- it's there in law already."

"If that happens," Mr. Jabavu said, "Africans will look to the east, first to India, then to China, and afterwards to Japan and the Soviet Union for their spiritual home. I say this deliberately and in no sense as an extremist."

"The colour bar in this country has made the non-white lose hope in western civilisation and feel that his destiny lies in eastern political power. I believe eventually the whole of Asia will be one unit, sentimentally and politically linked with Russia."

"As a fighter against the colour bar, I belong to a group aiming Marshalling non-whites, not in the hope of fighting physically against Europeans, but to get economic advantages and eventually to bring enough pressure on the Government to rescind the colour bar. 'We are struggling for absolute political equality, but by that I don't mean social mixing with whites. We are interested solely in the Capacity to live decently in our own home and develop in industry and professions now closed to us. We want appointments to important Government posts concerning our race."

Non-European Conference Plans of NIC

The Natal Indian Congress decided at its conference on Sunday to convene a South African conference of representatives of the various

Congress branches in the provinces of Natal, Transvaal and Cape Province within the shortest possible time at the most suitable venue.

The following proposals will be submitted for the consideration of the conference:

(a) The convention for a conference of non-European national organisation in South Africa:

(b) The inauguration of discussions between the various liberator' movements on the African Continents; and

(c) Request to the Indian National Congress to convene an All African-Asian Conference.

Before arriving at the decision the Congress carefully considered the constitutional position of the South African Congress, and the delay that is being caused by the appeal by the President and the Joint Secretaries of the SAIC against the Cape Supreme Court decision affecting the rights of the SAIC to hold meetings.

There was however a sharp cleavage of opinion of the competency of the Natal Indian Congress, to arrange such a conference. Some delegates felt that such a step would conflict with its terms of affiliation to the South African Congress.

Mr. Abdulla Moosa: Are we constitutionally competent ii'^ this conference?

Mr. J.N. Singh: it is within powers of the NIC to do so, further the people are looking forward to a lead from the NIC the largest constituent body of the South African Congress.

Mr. Debi Singh: The implications are grave and, therefore feel that this is a question which cannot be decided here in view our relations with the South African Indian Congress. I personally want more time to consider questions.

Mr. J.N. Singh felt that the NIC, despite what was said an independent body and so competent to convene the conference. It was decided to convene the conference. The details were left the executive committee of the NIC.

A face of fight

While historians are generally in agreement that the main anti-Indian feeling in South Africa was directed towards the merchant class, these sentiments were also directed against the "indentured" and "free" Indians. This was ironic as in the 1850s the Natal plantation owners desperately petitioned the Governor to introduce Indian labour. While people such as Harry Escombe, were stirring up anti-Indian feeling, there remained many other factors which influenced the Colonists. According to CG Henning, the following list of twenty anti-Indian attitudes compiled by him, contains real as well as imaginary complaints:

1. The withdrawal of grants of Crown Land (Act 25 of 1891) was meant to prevent Indians from settling in South Africa. Originally the colonists had hoped that nearly all the indentured Indians would either return to India or stay as re-indentured labourers on the plantations. As it turned out, very

few re-indentured and they began to settle in large numbers in Natal.

2. Act 17 of 1895 (the £3 tax) kept Indians in indenture; it made them return to India after five years labour (i.e., it assisted repatriation); and as the Indian contributed nothing towards income tax and the Colony's revenue, it was intended as "indirect taxation"65 just as the Black paid his annual "hut-tax." (The Act did not apply to Indians already domiciled at the time of the passing of the Act.)

3. Some White colonists believed that the Indian had been assisted to become richer and therefore was under obligation to return to India.

4. The Indian cultivator had succeeded in displacing nearly every White market gardener in the Colony.

5. The Whites were alarmed at the increase in the number of Indian landowners (farmers). In truth, only a small percentage purchased farms, the majority rented land.

6. "The 'free' Indians had taken over trades and occupations which previously had been the prerogative of the White man. This coupled with 4 and 5, above, may have brought about a

reduction by some "five thousand of the White population"67 and, . . . "by means of his rabbit-like fertility, the Indian has literally ousted the White man not only from his occupation, but literally from standing room."

7. According to Spencer Tyron, in the Zulu War of 1879 and in the Boer War, the Whites were capable of mustering a thousand (possibly more) volunteers to the defence of their country. The Indians contributed nothing towards the defence of the country, although this contribution in the form of the Stretcher Bearer Corps in 1900 was acknowledged.

8. The insanitary habits of the Indian peasants remained a long-standing grievance. It is possible that Indians introduced the bubonic plague, smallpox and other diseases.

9. The Indian was accused of outclassing the Zulu in crime. At one time "the Indians had the bulk of the illicit liquor traffic with the ?natives? in their hands.

10. The Indian belonged to a race which could not "amalgamate with the Whites by marriage."

11. The growing dislike of the Black towards the Indian caused racial friction.

12. The Black regarded the Indian as an undesirable competitor in the labour market.

13. The Whites objected to Natal becoming "a mere dumping ground for the refuse population of India."

14. The Indian population of Natal had increased considerably; by 1910 it was estimated to be about 130,000.

15. The Indian is a "very destructive and exhaustive cultivator." He neither manures, drains nor terraces hilly areas, and consequently after heavy rains, the soil is washed away *(a vindictive complaint).*

16. The Indian prefers "light" occupations, such as hawking or waiting in hotels, working in offices or in factories. There existed the possibility of a rising class of young educated Indians who were entering clerical work as posing a threat to the European Colonist. However, by 1914, there were still relatively few educated Indians.

17. As long as the Indian remained on the Estates, Durban Whites remained happy. However, as soon as the "free" Indians took to urbanisation and swelled Durban by becoming hawkers, artisans, market-gardeners and purchasing land, Durban's

Whites were alarmed because, . . . "They perceived the Africans as a passive threat and affected a paternal regard for their allegedly natural subordination, but eventually they saw in the Indians a sophisticated and active menace to their position in Colonial society, competing for space, place, trade and political influence with the Imperial authority. "

18. The imperialist factor however characterised White reasoning: "He does not consider he would be a good imperialist if he allowed any part of the Empire adapted to, and originally occupied by, a superior race, to be largely occupied by an inferior race, (and) the interests of White South Africa must not be subordinated to the general needs of the Empire." Expressed differently,

"The future of South Africa must forever be with the European races, governed by European ideas of government, and peopled by a race of Europeans . . . ". The force behind this motive being, "the natural instinct of self-preservation,"74 a factor which came to characterize the attitude of Whites towards all other inhabitants of South Africa.

19. Coming so soon after the Boer War, if Great Britain interfered too much in the affairs of self-governing states, she might possibly be faced with "a rebellion of both English and Dutch

Colonists." In other words, Great Britain would not be allowed to dictate or determine South Africa's future non-White policy. (This factor ultimately materialized in 1961 when the Union of South Africa declared itself a Republic outside the Commonwealth.)

20. A final factor which must be taken into account was that the years prior to 1910 witnessed great challenges in the development of Durban and other towns in Natal, which by now had already acquired a multi-national character with citizens from Europe, Africa and India. Maynard Swanson has made an interesting study of this aspect, which he sums up in these words:

"The towns (of Natal) thus emerged as the cockpits of communal conflict, and their municipalities stood forth as the protagonists of one racially defined segment of the community against the other, promoting baleful "solutions" to their common problems and their other Colonial rivalries."

Viewed in retrospect, the British concept of the great British Empire which was based on the concept of one monarch, with equality between all subjects, irrespective of race, creed or colour, was for its day a magnificent vision particularly if one takes into account the fact that India with its millions was part of this Empire. This concept formed the basis of all the Colonial territories. For example, according to the Natal Charter of 1856,

... "time expired Indians are in all respects free men, with rights and privileges not inferior to those of any class of the Queen's subjects in the Colony," recalled the Governor of Natal, Sir H. Bulwer.

When indentured Indian immigrants were transported to the various islands of the West Indies and the surrounding tropical areas, they were easily assimilated into their new communities. However, when they went to a predominantly White controlled Colony such as Natal, this great idealistic vision was doomed to failure. Perhaps the differences were not so much due to the mixture of races, but more for cultural, social and materialistic reasons. No one will deny the existence of strong racial prejudice between Whites and Indians at this particular period. At the Colonial Office the senior clerk for South Africa, Edward Fairfield, confirmed the prejudice when he remarked that . . . "The prejudice against Indians throughout South Africa, even in the Republics, is wholly English.

While Henry Polak condemned any type of discrimination outright, the Revd W. Pearson adopted a more sympathetic attitude and looked more objectively at the situation. The discrimination he attributed to "the conflict of civilisation" between the more complex 'civilisation of Western nations and the simpler ideals of the civilisation of the East. In South Africa the intense colour prejudice which existed he attributed firstly, "to the existence of a large native population which is four times as great as the White population" and secondly, to the evils of the indentured system which had produced "a lack of clear understanding or appreciation, of the great and ancient culture and civilisation of India, makes the White man in South Africa look upon the Indians in the same wayas he regards the native."

Pearson was intensely aware of the situation, one which has in fact plagued South African society up to the present day. In 1914 he wrote: 'This colour prejudice is the root cause of most of the grievances of the Indians at the present time. So long as it exists, it cannot be expected that the Indians will receive justice in political, social or legal matters. Christian principles do not seem to help in this matter, for very few of the Europeans seem to extend their Christianity so as to cover their relationships with coloured people. In this respect their Christianity is not even skin-deep."

As far as Natal was concerned, Pearson noted that "the Indian and European communities are mutually dependent on each other and benefit one another."82 The White for example cannot boycott the

Indian hawker "because it touches his pocket." On the other hand, the White's attitude should be more realistic: "I may make as much money out of him as I can, but I cannot tolerate the idea of his making any money out of me."

This is commercialism with colour prejudice added on and it is obvious that commercial rivalry was at the root of the new class struggle. Viewed in perspective the emergent new society of "free" Indians posed a threat to Whites from the poorer class, while the Indian merchant class posed a major threat to the wealthier White businessman.

Fortunately, Pearson in 1914 noted with pleasure the steadily rising standard of living, especially of the "free" Indians who, being in closer touch with the European community, were becoming more westernized. Indian children born in Natal were using English as the language of instruction and of communication. There was no question of Whites having to lower their standards; rather there was a gradual upliftment and advancement of the Indians. He personally advocated three factors which would go a long way towards establishing racial harmony:

- ➢ "a greater patience and tolerance on the part of the European;"

- ➤ "a greater sense of security of vested interests on the part of the Indian community"

- ➤ Indians "should conform to the European's ideas of cleanliness and sanitation."

Of special interest was Pearson's idea for improvement in education. He believed that ... "the disabilities which the Indians suffer can only be overcome by a persistent endeavour to show the Government their earnest desire for education up to a considerably higher standard than that at present generally amongst them."85

His recommendations remain noteworthy for 'self-help' projects, an aspect which has certainly come to distinguish the Indian community from any other group in South Africa during the first six decades of the twentieth century. In this respect, Pearson's advice reveals him to have been a man of far-sighted vision,

... "If the Indian community will itself lead the way by starting schools and asking for Government support, the education question will solve itself in time."

This remarkable prophesy certainly materialised with the establishment of "State-Aided Indian schools" and the establishment of Sastri College in 1930, the first Indian High School and Teacher

Training College. At one time three-quarters of Indian schools were State-Aided, and today there are about 450 educational institutions. Further, by means of a policy of "upliftment" and "improvement," the Indian by 1990 has, generally speaking, been able to raise his standards to reach the same socio-economic level as that of Whites.

The hostile attitude of the White Colonists in Natal (and to an even greater extent from the Whites in the Transvaal) brought about in turn, a complete disillusionment on the part of the Indians towards the administrative policies of His Majesty's Government. Fortunately they retained a strong loyalty to the Crown and to the Empire because,

"the uneducated Indians look upon their Sovereign as their all-powerful protector. They believe in the divine right of kings. They know nothing of constitutions or self-government. So far as they are concerned, the only personality that exists in the political world is that of their Emperor." 87

It must be remembered that the indentured Indian labourer was invited to come to Natal and up to 1891, was even offered grants of land. Thereafter, they realised with dismay that British Natal did not want "free-passenger" Indians or "free" Indians but that the "indentured Indian labourer is warmly welcomed because he does work which a White man would not stoop to perform." Opportunities in the less-crowded Colonies were better than in India and a return to India, may mean a life of penury.

The series of restrictive laws passed in Natal revealed strong anti-Indian feeling. The Indian wanted to be "treated on terms of perfect equality with the White subjects of the British Sovereign." As far as they were concerned, the British in Natal had broken their promises, because as British subjects it was difficult to purchase land or trade freely in any area; further, discriminatory practices prevented them from obtaining lucrative employment.

The Government and the people of India took a very dim view of the situation, but what alarmed them the most were the reports during the first decade of the twentieth century, of the so-called ill-treatment and irregularities which were committed against their Indian compatriots in Natal. This, perhaps more than any other factor, hastened the end of the period of indenture

Indian Regulation Struggle

Towards the end of the nineteenth century, Harry Escombe became one of the most prominent White politicians in the Colony of Natal. Initially he pursued a policy of moderation towards the Indians. Escombe was in favour of the Wragg Commission being appointed to investigate Indian immigration laws, yet six years later he became one of the strongest opponents of Indian immigration into the Colony of Natal. Bills were introduced into the Natal Legislative Assembly with the intention of curbing Indian immigration. The Indian Immigration Trust Board Amendment Bill, with the object of discontinuing the annual grant of £10 000 for the transportation of Indian immigrants, was introduced to prevent public money being spent in this way. Escombe was of the opinion that the planters should import labour at their own expense. However, the planters rejected his proposal in the Assembly.

Anti-Indian feelings became stronger with every passing year, e.g., Escombe said, This country (Natal) was meant for Europeans and was never intended to be an Asiatic Colony.

As part of the anti-Indian campaign, laws were passed to this effect. The first law was Act 25 of 1891. Act 25 of 1894 followed by Act 8 of 1896 disenfranchised about 251 Asiatics of the vote.

In 1893, the Colony of Natal sent a deputation consisting of L. Mason and H.Binns to India to negotiate a new agreement for the conditions of indenture to Natal. As a result Act 17 of 1895, the Indian Immigration Law Amendment Bill, was promulgated on 18 August 1896 which decreed that:

- After a five year period of indenture, the Indian had to return to India. Alternately, they had to re-indenture. However desperate poverty made most of them accept 10 shillings per month, the maximum salary being 20 shillings per month.

- Should the Indian desire to remain in the Colony of Natal, a penalty of £3 tax per annum had to be paid, in addition to an annual £1 tax for males. This tax became operative around 1902.

The residential tax of £3 per annum proved to be extremely unpopular with the ex-indentured workers. It imposed an unfair burden on Indians, who in the majority of cases were too poor to pay it. The Government of India was alarmed at this legislation and the two governments hotly debated this subject. In 1903, the tax was extended to girls aged 13 and boys aged 16. As a result by 1911, thousands of people were in debt and an explosive situation was created with Gandhi intervening, resulting in the tax being withdrawn.

Between 15 October 1896 and 4 January 1897, the *SS Courland* and the *SS Naderi* brought an additional 500 to 600 free passenger Indians. A hue and cry followed. Public meetings were held and various telegrams were sent to the Colonial Secretary to prevent the lading of any more free Indians in the Colony and that those who had just arrived should be sent back to India. Around 8 January, a 5 000 strong crowd held a noisy demonstration at the Point in Durban.

At the next session of Parliament, Escombe piloted the Immigration Restriction Bill, Act 1 of 1897. The purpose of the Bill was to stop the "threatened evil" or menace of an Asiatic invasion of Natal. The protestors demanded that the matter be raised at a special session of Parliament. Escombe argued that, "We claim the right as British citizens, to say, This Colony is not open to you." The aim was to restrict the growth of the Indian population in Natal, especially that of the merchant class. In the same year, the Dealer's Licences Amendment Bill (No. 18 of 1897) also became law and added to the plight of merchant class Indians.

In 1903, the government of Natal sent a second delegation comprised of HE Shepstone and CB de Gersigny to India to discuss subsequent immigration to the Colony which included formulating new and revised conditions of service for new intending Indian immigrants. Prior to their departure, FR Moor, the acting Prime Minister of Natal stated that the object of their mission was to secure an increased recruitment of 15 000 Indian labourers for Natal. Demand for Indian labour had increased considerably since they were now employed outside the sugar industry.

Basically, the Whites in Natal held three grievances against further Indian arrivals:

- The first was the steady rise in Indian population. By 1901, it was estimated that the Indian population of Natal was 81 965
- The second issue was that with the ex-indentured Indian, repatriation was very unpopular. In the period 1896 to 1901, only 8% returned to India

- The third grievance was the failure of the £3 tax to increase repatriation coupled with a substantial increase in re-indenture

In the eyes of the Natal Colonists, the 1895 laws proved a failure because they attempted to encourage repatriation and increase re-indenture but reduce the number of Indian settlers

The grievances of the Natal Indian Trust Board were:

The antagonism of the Labour Party, which was strenuously opposed to any increase in the free Indian population and would not hesitate to prohibit immigration altogether

Gandhi and the Passive Struggle Campaign 1907-1914

The passive resistance campaigns led by MK Gandhi in South Africa had huge consequences not only for the history of the country but also for world history in general. Gandhi's campaigns forged a new form of struggle against oppression that became a model for political and ethical struggles in other parts of the world – especially in India (the struggle for independence) and the United States (the civil rights campaign of the 1960s).

Gandhi himself was transformed by the struggles he waged: his first battles for the rights of a small group of Indians in South Africa eventually broadened his outlook into a more universal struggle for human rights. From a representative of a small faction of one ethnic group Gandhi was forced by the logic of his 'experiments with truth' to become a defender of the rights of the oppressed and downtrodden. Yet for some critics he was too constrained by the limits of his middle-class formation and failed to generalise his commitment to a truly universal philosophy of human rights.

Gandhi, as Maureen Swan has demonstrated, was not the initiator of Indian political activity in Natal and South Africa. Indian traders and middle classes had already formed associations to represent their interests before Gandhi arrived in South Africa.

It was around 1904 that Gandhi began to think about his 'duty' to the wider community, and not just to his clients, although Swan argues that at that time Gandhi was still thinking about the wider middle classes, and not indentured labourers or non-Indians. She writes: 'By 1904, however, he had begun to develop the humanistic, universalist political philosophy out of which passive resistance grew. But Gandhi's politics lagged behind his ideology. The first passive resistance campaign was started in Johannesburg in 1907 with, and for, the wealthy South African Indian merchants whom he had so long represented.'

Gandhi's first passive resistance campaign began as a protest against the Asiatic Registration Bill of 1906. The bill was part of the attempt to limit the presence of Indians in the Transvaal by confining them to segregated areas and limiting their trading activities.

Indians in South Africa

Indians first arrived in South Africa in 1860 as indentured labourers. Between then and 1911, 152,000 Indians had come to work on the sugar estates, most of them from Calcutta and Madras. After 1890 Indians also began to work on the railways and in coal mines. By the turn of the century, there were about 30,000 indentured workers in Natal, and before the Anglo-Boer War a few thousand had moved to the Transvaal.

By the 1880s, some Indians began to open shops or trade as hawkers, a development perceived as a threat by Whites, especially in Natal, where the Wragg Commission of 1885-7 found that Indian traders were responsible for 'much of the irritation existing in the minds of European Colonists'. After Natal was granted self-government in 1893, the government passed a series of laws discriminating against Indians, requiring them to undergo literacy tests, keep accounts in English, and denying them the vote.

After 1895, the workers who had completed their terms of indenture had to pay a tax if they wanted to remain in the country. They were required by law to pay a tax of Â£3 a year for each member of the family – a huge amount of money at the time. This measure was aimed at pushing people back into indentured labour and encouraged them to return to India.

After 1903/4 Indians were no longer allowed to work in the gold mines on the Rand and opportunities to earn the money to pay the taxes were severely limited. By the middle of the decade, many Indians were severely in debt and went back into new contracts as indentured labourers. They were poorly paid, lived in squalid conditions and death rates were high.

Working conditions were better in coal mines and on the railways, but in the sugar plantations strict control of the workforce meant they could not organise themselves into unions – workers were not allowed to leave their places of employment without written leave, which was rarely given. Strikes were spontaneous and short-lived, and more often workers resorted to other forms of resistance, such as absenteeism, desertion, petty theft or sabotage.

While an Indian elite (made up mostly of Muslim businessmen) already existed, a new elite also emerged from among the Tamil workforce, most of them the children of freed indentured labourers – this new group numbered 300 in a 1904 census. Most of these were salaried white-collar workers - some teachers, small farmers and entrepreneurs, but also lawyers, civil servants and accountants in the mix.

By the late 19th century, Indians had spread to the four colonies that would become the Union of South Africa in 1910, and whites in all of these colonies perceived them as a threat. Governments in all the colonies enacted laws to limit Indian rights to reside and trade. They were required to carry passes and after 1898 were even forbidden to walk on pavements.

Mohandas Karamchand Gandhi

Early life and education

Mohandas Karamchand Gandhi was born to a Hindu family on 2 October 1869, in Porbandar, Gujarat, India. He was the last child of Karamchand Gandhi, his father and his father's fourth wife Putlibai. His father belonged to the merchant caste. His early schooling was in nearby Rajkot, where his father served as the adviser or prime minister to the local ruler. India was then under British rule. His father died before Gandhi could finish his schooling. At thirteen, the young Gandhi was married to Kasturba [or Kasturbai], who was of the same age as himself. She bore him four sons.

In September 1888 Gandhi set sail for England, to pursue a degree in law. Gandhi left behind his son Harilal, then a few months old. He spent three years stay in London being a serious student, living a very simple lifestyle. He became deeply interested in vegetarianism and study of different religions. His stay in England provided opportunities for widening horizons and better understanding of religions and cultures.

Gandhi successfully completed his degree at the Inner Temple and was called to the Bar on 10 June 1891. He enrolled in the High Court of London; but later that year he left for India. For the next two years, Gandhi attempted to practice law in India, establishing himself in the legal profession in Bombay. Unfortunately, he found that he lacked both knowledge of Indian law and self-confidence at trial. His practice collapsed and he returned home to Porbandar. It was while he was contemplating his seemingly bleak future that a representative of an Indian business firm situated in the Transvaal (now Gauteng), South Africa offered him employment. He was to work in South Africa for a period of 12 months for a fee of £105.00.

Gandhi in South Africa

Gandhi arrived in Durban, Natal (now kwaZulu-Natal) in 1893 to serve as legal counsel to a merchant Dada Abdulla. In June, Dada Abdulla asked him to undertake a rail trip to Pretoria, Transvaal, a journey which first took Gandhi to Pietermaritzburg, Natal. There, Gandhi was seated in the first-class compartment, as he had purchased a first-class ticket. A White person who entered the compartment hastened to summon the White railway officials, who ordered Gandhi to remove himself to the van compartment, since 'coolies' (a racist term for Indians) and non-whites were not permitted in first-class compartments.

Gandhi protested and produced his ticket, but was warned that he would be forcibly removed if he did not make a gracious exit. As Gandhi refused to comply with the order, a White police officer pushed him out of the train, and his luggage was tossed out on to the platform. The train steamed away, and Gandhi withdrew to the waiting room. "It was winter," Gandhi was to write in his autobiography, and "the cold was extremely bitter. My overcoat was in my luggage, but I did not dare to ask for it lest I should be insulted again, so I sat and shivered". He says he began to think of his "duty": ought he to stay back and fight for his "rights", or should he return to India? His own "hardship was superficial", "only a symptom of the deep disease of colour prejudice."

The next evening he continued the train journey-this time without a mishap. But a bigger mishap awaited him on the journey from Charlestown to Johannesburg which had to be covered by stagecoach. He was made to sit with the coachman on the box outside, while the white conductor sat inside with the white passengers.

Gandhi pocketed the insult for fear of missing the coach altogether. On the way the conductor who wanted a smoke spread a piece of dirty sack-cloth on the footboard and ordered Gandhi to sit there so that the conductor could have Gandhi's seat and smoke. Gandhi refused. The conductor swore and rained blows on him, trying to throw him down. Gandhi clung to the brass rails of the coach box, refusing to yield and unwilling to retaliate. Some of the White passengers protested at this cowardly assault and the conductor was obliged to stop beating Gandhi who kept his seat.

The position of Indians in the Transvaal was worse than in Natal. They were compelled to pay a poll tax of £3; they were not allowed to own land except in specially allotted locations, a kind of ghetto; they had no franchise, and were not allowed to walk on the pavement or move out of doors after 9 p.m. without a special permit. One day Gandhi, who had received from the State Attorney a letter authorizing him to be out of doors all hours, was having his usual walk. As he passed near President Kruger's house, the policeman on duty, suddenly and without any warning, pushed him off the pavement and kicked him into the street. A Mr. Coates, an English Quaker, who knew Gandhi, happened to pass by and saw the incident. He advised Gandhi to proceed against the man and offered himself as witness. But Gandhi declined the offer saying that he had made it a rule not to go to court in respect of a personal grievance.

During his stay in Pretoria, Gandhi read about 80 books on religion. He came under the influence of Christianity but refused to embrace it. During this period, Gandhi attended Bible classes.

Within a week of his arrival there, Gandhi made his first public speech making truthfulness in business his theme. The meeting was called to awaken the Indian residents to a sense of the oppression they were suffering under. He took up the issue of Indians in regard to first class travel in railways. As a result, an assurance was given that first and second-class tickets would be issued to Indians "who were properly dressed". This was a partial victory.

These incidents lead Gandhi to develop the concept of Satyagraha. He united the Indians from different communities, languages and religions, who had settled in South Africa.

By the time Gandhi arrived in South Africa the growing national- perpetuated by the White ruling authorities and the majority of the White citizenry - anti-Indian attitude had spread to Natal (now kwaZulu-Natal). The first discriminatory legislation directed at Indians, Law 3 of 1885, was passed in the South African Republic, or the Transvaal. The right to self-government had been granted to Natal in

1893 and politicians were increasing pressure to pass legislation aimed at containing the 'merchant [Indian] menace'.

Two bills were passed in the following two years restricting the freedom of Indians severely. The Immigration Law Amendment Bill stated that any Indian had to return to India at the end of a five-year indenture period or had to be re-indentured for a further two years. If he refused an amount of £3 annual tax had to be paid. The bill came into law in 1895. A Franchise Amendment Bill was introduced in 1894. It was designed to limit the franchise to Indians who had the vote. Although there were only 300 of them, in comparison to 10 000 white voters, the Bill caused outrage among Indian leadership. They decided to contest the measure by any means available to them.

Having completed his work in Pretoria, Gandhi returned to Durban and prepared to sail home. At a farewell dinner, in April 1894, given in his honour someone showed him a news item in the Natal Mercury that the Natal Government proposed to introduce a bill to disfranchise Indians. Gandhi immediately understood the ominous implications of this bill which, as he said, "is the first nail into our coffin" and advised his compatriots to resist it by concerned action. But they pleaded their helplessness without him and begged him to stay on for another month. He agreed little realizing that this one month would grow into twenty years.

Gandhi immediately turned the farewell dinner into a meeting and an action committee was formed. This committee then drafted a petition to the Natal Legislative Assembly. Volunteers came forward to make copies of the petition and to collect signatures - all during the night. The petition received much favourable publicity in the press the following morning. The bill was however passed. Undeterred, Gandhi set to work on another petition to Lord Ripon, the Secretary of State for Colonies. Within a month the mammoth petition with ten thousand signatures was sent to Lord Ripon and a thousand copies printed for distribution. Even The Times admitted the justice of the Indian claim and for the first time the people in India came to know of the oppressive lot of their compatriots in South Africa.

Gandhi insisted that if he had to extend his stay in South Africa he would accept no remuneration for his public services and since he still thought it necessary to live as befitted a barrister he needed about £300 to meet his expenses. He therefore enrolled as an advocate of the Supreme Court of Natal.

On 25 June 1894, at the residence of Sheth Abdulla, with Sheth Haji Muhammad, the foremost Indian leader of Natal in the chair, a meeting of Indians was held and it was resolved to offer opposition to the Franchise Bill. Here Gandhi outlined his plan of action to oppose this bill.

Gandhi played a prominent role in the planned campaign. As a talented letter-writer and meticulous planner, he was assigned the task of compiling all petitions, arranging meetings with politicians and addressing letters to newspapers. He also campaigned in India and made an, initially, successful appeal to the British Secretary of State for the Colonies, Lord Ripon. He was instrumental in the formation of theNatal Indian Congress (NIC) on 22 August 1894, which marked the birth of the first permanent political organisation to strive to maintain and protect the rights of Indians in South Africa.

By 1896 Gandhi had established himself as a political leader in South Africa. In this year, he undertook a journey to India to launch a protest campaign on behalf of Indians in South Africa. It took the form of letters written to newspapers, interviews with leading nationalist leaders and a number of public meetings. His mission caused great uproar in India and consternation among British authorities in England and Natal. Gandhi embarrassed the British Government enough to cause it to block the Franchise Bill in an unprecedented move, which resulted in anti-Indian feelings in Natal reaching dangerous new levels.

While in India, an urgent telegram from the Indian community in Natal obliged him to cut short his stay. He set sail for Durban with his wife and children on 30 November 1896. Gandhi did not realize that while he had been away from South Africa, his pamphlet of Indian grievances, known as the Green Pamphlet, had been exaggerated and distorted. When the ship reached Durban harbour, it was for held for 23 days in quarantine. The European community, misled by garbled versions of Gandhi's activities in India and by a rumour that he was bringing shiploads of Indians to settle in Natal, were wild with anger and threatened to drown all the passengers.

News of this cowardly assault received wide publicity and Joseph Chamberlain, the British Secretary of States for the Colonies, cabled an order to Natal to prosecute all those who were responsible for the attempted lynching. However, Gandhi refused to identify and prosecute his assailants, saying that they were misled and that he was sure that when they came to know the truth they would be sorry for what they had done.

It was during this second period in South Africa that Gandhi's underwent a gradual change. Previously he was anxious to maintain the standard of an English barrister. Now he began, to methodically reduce his wants and his expenses. He began to do his own laundry and clean out his own chamber-pots but often his guests as well.

Not satisfied with self-help, he volunteered, despite his busy practice as a lawyer and demand of public work, his free service for two hours a day at a charitable hospital. He also undertook the education at home of his two sons and a nephew. He read books on nursing and midwifery and in fact served as midwife when his fourth and last son was born in Natal.

In 1899 the Second Anglo-Boer (South African War) war broke out. Though Gandhi's sympathies were with the Boers who were fighting for their independence, he advised the Indian community to support the British cause, on the ground that since they claimed their rights as British subjects, it was their duty to defend the Empire when it was threatened. He organized and, with the help of a Dr. Booth, trained an Indian Ambulance Corps of 1,100 volunteers and offered its services to the Government. The corps under Gandhi's leadership rendered valuable service and was mentioned in dispatches.

In 1901, at the end of the war, Gandhi wanted to return to India. His professional success in South Africa might, he feared turn him into a "money-maker". With great difficulty he persuaded his friends to let him go and promised to return should the community need him within a year.

He reached India in time to attend the Calcutta session of the Indian National Congress and had the satisfaction of seeing his resolution on South Africa pass with acclamation. He was however disappointed with the congress. He felt that Indian politicians talked too much but did little.

Hardly had he set up in practice in Bombay when a cablegram from the Indian community in Natal recalled him. He had given them his word that he would return if needed. Leaving his family in India he sailed again.

He had been called to put the Indian case before Joseph Chamberlain who was visiting South Africa. But the Colonial Secretary who had come to receive a gift of thirty-five million pounds from South Africa had no intention to alienate the European community. Gandhi failed in his mission to win Chamberlain's sympathy and discovered in the process that the situation in the Transvaal had become ominous for the Indians. He therefore decided to stay on in Johannesburg and enrolled as an advocate of the Supreme Court.

Though he stayed on specifically to challenge White arrogance and to resist injustice, he harboured no hatred in his heart and was in fact always ready to help when they were in distress. It was this rare combination of readiness to resist wrong and capacity to love his opponent which baffled his enemies and compelled their admiration.

When the Zulu rebellion broke out, he again offered his help to the Government and raised an Indian Ambulance Corps. He was happy that he and his men had to nurse the sick and dying Zulus whom the White doctors and nurses were unwilling to touch.

Gandhi was involved in the formation British Indian Association (BIA) in 1903. The movement was to prevent proposed evictions of Indians in the Transvaal under British leadership. According to Arthur Lawley, the newly appointed Lieutenant Governor Lord Alfred Milner said that Whites were to be protected against Indians in what he called a 'struggle between East and West for the inheritance of the semi-vacant territories of South Africa'.

Satyagraha

Influenced by the Hindu religious book, the Bhagvad Gita, Gandhi wanted to purify his life by following the concepts of aparigraha (non-possession) and samabhava (equability). A friend gave him the book, Unto This Last, by John Ruskin; Gandhi became excited about the ideals proffered by Ruskin. The book inspired Gandhi to establish a communal living community called Phoenix Settlement just outside of Durban in June 1904. The Settlement was an experiment in communal living, a way to eliminate one's needless possessions and to live in a society with full equality. Gandhi moved his newspaper, the Indian Opinion , established in June 1903 and its workers to the Phoenix Settlement as well as his own family a bit later. Besides a building for the press, each community member was allotted three acres of land on which to build a dwelling made of corrugated iron. In addition to farming, all members of the community were to be trained and expected to help with the newspaper.

In 1906, believing that family life was taking away from his full potential as a public advocate, Gandhi took the vow of brahmacharya (a vow of abstinence against sexual relations, even with one's own wife). This was not an easy vow for him to follow, but one that he worked diligently to keep for the rest of his life. Thinking that one passion fed others, Gandhi decided to restrict his diet in order to remove passion from his palette. To aid him in this endeavour, Gandhi simplified his diet from strict vegetarianism to foods that were unspiced and usually uncooked, with fruits and nuts being a large portion of his food choices. Fasting, he believed, would also help still the urges of the flesh.

Gandhi believed that his taking the vow of brahmacharya had allowed him the focus to come up with the concept of Satyagraha in late 1906. In the very simplest sense, Satyagraha is passive resistance. However, Gandhi believed the English phrase of "passive resistance" did not represent the true spirit of Indian resistance since passive resistance was often thought to be used by the weak and was a tactic that could potentially be conducted in anger.

Needing a new term for the Indian resistance, Gandhi chose the term "satyagraha," which literally means "truth force." Since Gandhi believed that exploitation was only possible if both the exploited and the exploiter accepted it, if one could see above the current situation and see the universal truth, then one had the power to make change. (Truth, in this manner, could mean "natural right," a right granted by nature and the universe that should not be impeded on by man.)

In practice, Satyagraha was a focused and forceful nonviolent resistance to a particular injustice. A Satyagrahi (a person using Satyagraha) would resist the injustice by refusing to follow an unjust law. In doing so, he would not be angry, would put up freely with physical assaults to his person and the confiscation of his property, and would not use foul language to smear his opponent. A practitioner of Satyagraha also would never take advantage of an opponent's problems. The goal was not for there to be a winner and loser of the battle, but rather, that all would eventually see and understand the "truth" and agree to rescind the unjust law.

On 28 December 1907 the first arrests of Indians refusing to register were made, and by the end of January 1908, 2000 Asians had been jailed. Gandhi had also been jailed several times, but many key figures in the movement fled the colony rather than be arrested. .

The first time Gandhi officially used Satyagraha was in South Africa beginning in 1907 when he organised opposition to the Asiatic Registration Law (the Black Act). In March 1907, the Black Act was passed, requiring all Indians - young and old, men and women - to get fingerprinted and to keep registration documents on them at all times. Gandhi advised the Indian community to refuse to submit to this indignity and to court imprisonment by defying the law. Indians refused to get fingerprinted and picketed the documentation offices.

Mass protests were organised, miners went on strike, and masses of Indians travelled, illegally, from Natal to the Transvaal in opposition to the Black Act. Many of the protesters were beaten and arrested. In January 1908, he was arrested and sentenced to two months' simple imprisonment. He was followed by other Satyagrahis. This was the first of Gandhi's many jail sentences. It took seven years of protest, before the Black Act was repealed in June 1914. Gandhi had proved that nonviolent protest could be immensely successful.

The Indians made a bonfire of their registration certificates and decided to defy the ban on immigration to the Transvaal. Jails began to be filled. Gandhi was arrested a second time in September 1908 and sentenced to two months' imprisonment, this time hard labour. The struggle continued. In February 1909 he was arrested a third time and sentenced to three months' hard labour. He made such good use of his time in jail with study and prayer that he was able to declare that "the real road to ultimate happiness lies in going to jail and undergoing sufferings and privations there in the interest of one's own country and religion".

Before the prison term was over General Jan Smuts sent him an emissary proposed that if the Indians voluntarily registered themselves he promised to repeal the Act. Gandhi and the leader of the Chinese population in South Africa, Leung Quin, agreed to the compromise. He always believed in trusting the opponent, but other Indians were not so trusting. One burly Indian, a Pathan, even charged Gandhi with having betrayed them and threatened to kill him if he registered. On the day Gandhi went out to register he was waylaid and attacked by this and other Pathans and severely injured. When he recovered consciousness and was told that his assailants had been arrested he insisted on them being released.

Gandhi registered, but his disappointment was great when Smuts went back on his word and refused to repeal the Black Act along with denying any promises were made. The Indians made a bonfire of their registration certificates and decided to defy the ban. In June 1909, he left for London after having defended his position as leader of the Transvaal merchant community

Gandhi returned to South Africa in December 1909 to find that members of the NIC were openly plotting against him. He was fighting for his political survival and withdrew to Tolstoy, a farm he had purchased in 1910 to support the families of jailed passive resisters. Gandhi only came under the public eye again in 1912 as a result of a visit to South Africa by Indian statesman Gopal Krishna Gokhale. He was accused of preventing opponents of his policies to speak with the visitor and finally, on 26 April 1913 Gandhi and his rivals in the NIC went their separate ways.

In 1911, a provisional settlement of the Asiatic question in the Transvaal brought about a suspension of the Satyagraha campaign. In the following year, Gokhale visited South Africa and on the eve of his departure assured Gandhi that the Union Government had promised to repeal the Black Act, to remove the racial bar from the immigration law and to abolish the £3 tax. But Gandhi had his fears which were soon borne out. The Union Government went back on its promise, and to this fire was added a very powerful fuel when a judgment of the Supreme Court ruled that only Christian marriages were legal in South Africa, turning at one stroke all Indian marriages in South Africa invalid and all Indian wives into concubines. This provoked Indian women, including, Kasturbai, to join the struggle.

It was illegal for the Indians to cross the border from the Transvaal into Natal, and vice versa, without a permit. Indian women from the Tolstoy Ashram, which Gandhi set up in the Transvaal, crossed the border without permits and proceeded to Newcastle to persuade the Indian miners there to strike. They succeeded and were arrested. The strike spread and thousands of miners and other Indians prepared, under Gandhi's leadership, to march to the Transvaal border in a concerted act of non-violent defiance.

On the 29th October, 1913, hundreds of men, women and children led by Gandhi marched from Newcastle, Natal Colony (now KwaZulu Natal) into the Transvaal to purposefully defy the Immigrants Regulation Act of 1913 (Act no. 22). Gandhi was followed by two parties led by Thambi Naidoo and Albert Christopher. This marked one of the greatest episodes in South African history. He was arrested the following day at Palmford. Prior to this march, Thambi Naidoo mobilised the Indian community at Newcastle to start the Satyagraha Campaign (Passive Resistance Campaign).Gandhi made strict rules for the conduct of the Satyagrahis who were to submit patiently and without retaliation to insult, flogging or arrest. While leading a march on 6 November 1913, which included 127 women, 57 children and 2037 men, Gandhi was arrested. He was released on bail, rejoined the march and was re-arrested. The Indian Relief Bill was finally scrapped.

At one time there were about fifty thousand indentured labourers on strike and several thousand other Indians in jail. The Government tried repression and even shooting, and many lives were lost. "In the end", as an American biographer has put it, "General Smuts did what every Government that ever opposed Gandhi had to do - he yielded."

A spontaneous strike by Indians in Natal altered the situation radically. Here violent confrontation ruled and several strikers were killed and injured in clashes with the police and more protesters joined. By the end of November 1913 produce markets in Durban and Pietermaritzburg had come to a standstill, sugar mills were closed and hotels, restaurants and homes were left without domestic workers. Reports in India relating the arrest of Gandhi and police brutality caused uproar and the British government was forced to form an agreement with the strikers.

Gandhi was released in order to negotiate with Smuts over the Indian Relief Bill, a law that scrapped the £3 tax on ex-indentured workers. The law was scrapped.

Gandhi was released and, in January 1914, a provisional agreement was arrived at between him and General Smuts and the main Indian demands were conceded. Gandhi's work in South Africa was now over and, in July 1914, he sailed with his wife for England. Before sailing, he sent a pair of sandals he had made in jail to General Smuts as a gift.

Recalling the gift twenty-five years later, the General wrote:

I have worn these sandals for many a summer since then even though I may feel that I am not worthy to stand in the shoes of so great a man."

Return to India

Having spent twenty years in South Africa helping fight discrimination, Gandhi decided it was time to head back to India in July 1914. On his way home, Gandhi was scheduled to make a short stop in England. However, when World War I broke out during his journey, Gandhi decided to stay in England and form another ambulance corps of

Indians to help the British. When the British air caused Gandhi to take ill, he sailed to India in January 1915.

Gandhi's struggles and triumphs in South Africa had been reported in the worldwide press. By the time he reached home, in India, he was a national hero. Although he was eager to begin reforms in India, a friend advised him to wait a year and spend the time travelling around India to acquaint himself with the people and their tribulations.

Yet Gandhi soon found his fame getting in the way of accurately seeing the conditions that the poorer people lived in day to day. In an attempt to travel more anonymously, Gandhi began wearing a loincloth (dhoti) and sandals (the average dress of the masses) during this journey. If it was cold out, he would add a shawl. This became his wardrobe for the rest of his life.

Also during this year of observation, Gandhi founded another communal settlement, this time in Ahmadabad and called the Sabarmati Ashram. Gandhi lived on the Ashram for the next sixteen years, along with his family and several members who had once been part of the Phoenix Settlement.

The title 'Mahatma'

It was during his first year back in India that Gandhi was given the honorary title of Mahatma ("Great Soul"). Many credit Indian poet Rabindranath Tagore, winner of the 1913 Nobel Prize for Literature, for both awarding Gandhi of this name and of publicising it. The title represented the feelings of the millions of Indian peasants who viewed Gandhi as a holy man. However, Gandhi never liked the title because it seemed to mean he was special while he viewed himself as ordinary.

However other sources claim it was Nagar Sheth of Jetpur, Shri Nautamlal B. Mehta (Kamdar), who was the first to use and bestow "Mahatma" for Mohandas Karamchand Gandhi on 21 January 1915 at Kamri Bai School, Jetpur, India. From then on, Gandhi was known as Mahatma Gandhi. It is commonly believed that Rabindranath Tagore first bestowed the name. However, this is incorrect.

On 30 January 1948, Gandhi hurriedly went up the few steps of the prayer ground in a large park in Delhi. He had been detained by a conference with the Deputy Prime Minister, Sardar Vallabhbhai Patel, and was late by a few minutes. He loved punctuality and was worried that he had kept the congregation waiting. "I am late by ten minutes," he murmured. "I should be here at the stroke of five." He raised his hands and touched the palms together to greet the crowd that was waiting.

Every one returned the greeting. Many came forward wanting to touch his feet. They were not allowed to do so, as Gandhi was already late. But a young Hindu from Poona, Nathuram Vinayak Godse, forced his way forward and while seeming to do obeisance fired three point-blank shots from a small automatic pistol aimed at the heart. Gandhi fell, his lips uttering the name of God (He Ram). Before medical aid could arrive the heart had ceased to beat.

Satyagraha: the first campaign

After the victory of the British in the Anglo-Boer War (1899-1902), Indians in the Transvaal had hoped that the British administration would treat them more favourably, but the British instead passed a string of laws to limit the rights of Indians. In August 1906 the Transvaal Government Gazette published a draft of a new law which made it compulsory for all Indian males above the age of eight to be registered and have their fingerprints taken and recorded. Gandhi said the law would spell 'absolute ruin for the Indians of South Africa"¦ Better to die than submit to such a law'.

Now Gandhi began to clarify his concept of passive resistance, outlining its rationale. He disliked the notion of passivity, and called for people to come up with an appropriate name for the new mode of resistance. When his nephew made a suggestion, Sadagraha (firmness in a good cause), Gandhi adapted the idea and coined the word 'Satyagraha', which means 'truth force'.

Gandhi biographer Louis Fischer says Satyagraha 'means to be strong not with the strength of the brute but with the strength of the spark of God'. Satyagraha, according to Gandhi, is 'the vindication of truth not by infliction of suffering on the opponent but on one's self'. The intention is to convince the opponent and not to crush him, to convert the opponent, who must be 'weaned from error by patience and sympathy'.

Before the law came into force, Gandhi organised a mass meeting on 11 September 1906 at the Imperial Theatre in Johannesburg, where 3000 people pledged to defy the law – a short while later this would develop into the first passive resistance campaign. On 20 September 1906, the Crown government passed the Asiatic Law Amendment Ordinance No. 29, which became known as the 'Black Act'.

Gandhi went to London in October to appeal to the British to abolish the Black Act in their crown colony of Transvaal, and met with the Secretary of State for the Colonies, Lord Elgin, and John Morley, Secretary of State for India, addressing MPs in a committee room of the House of Commons.

The British vetoed the law in December 1906, while Gandhi was on a ship returning to South Africa. But the British granted the Transvaal self-government from 1 January 1907, leaving the new administration under General Louis Botha free to re-enact the law, this time as the Transvaal Registration Act. The law eventually came into force on 31 July 1907, after the British government approved the act on 9 May 1907.

On 11 May Gandhi announced that Indians would embark on their campaign against the Black Act.

The First Campaign

Of the 13,000 Indians in the Transvaal, only 511 had registered by the last day of registration, 30 November 1907 – the campaign was thus underway, with the majority refusing to register.

Indians were served with official notices to register or leave the Transvaal and Gandhi was arrested on 27 December. Gandhi and a group of resisters appeared before a magistrate on 11 January 1908. He appealed to the judge to be given the heaviest sentence, and he was sentenced to a term of two months. Four other Satyagrahis were jailed with Gandhi and by 29 January the figure had risen to 155.

In jail, Gandhi spent his time reading Ruskin, Tolstoy and the holy books of various religions – the *Baghavad Gita* and the *Qur'an*. He was approached by Albert Cartwright, editor of the *Transvaal Leader*, on behalf of Jan Smuts. Cartwright promised that if Gandhi and his supporters registered voluntarily, the Black Act would be repealed.

Gandhi met with Smuts on 30 January, the agreement was formalised and he was immediately set free. The other resisters were released the next morning.

The agreement with Smuts drew criticisms from some passive resisters. They wanted the act repealed before they would register, but Gandhi saw the move as the way of the Satyagrahi. He said: 'A Satyagrahi bids goodbye to fear. He is therefore never afraid of trusting the opponent. Even if the opponent plays him false twenty times, the Satyagrahi is ready to trust him for the 21st time – for an implicit trust in human nature is the very essence of his creed.'

At a public meeting, Gandhi, cognisant of the predicament of his opponents, explained to the community that Smuts was under pressure from whites to limit Indian immigration, and that a voluntary registration would leave room for the state to treat all citizens equally. This way, Indians would not be bowing to force, which took away from their dignity. Voluntary registration would indicate to the state that the Indians would not bring other Indians into the Transvaal illegally and would place an obligation on the state to treat all equally.

A huge and fierce Pathan member of the community accused Gandhi of having sold out the community for £15,000. He swore that he would not allow himself to be fingerprinted and would kill anyone who voluntarily agreed to fingerprinting. Gandhi answered that he would be the first to be fingerprinted, saying: 'Death is the appointed end of all life. To die by the hand of a brother, rather than by disease or in such other way, cannot be for me a matter of sorrow. And if, even in such a case, I am free from the thought of anger or hatred against my assailant, I know that that will redound to my eternal welfare, and even the assailant will later on realise my perfect innocence.'

On the morning of 10 February, Gandhi went to his office, where a group of large Pathans had gathered outside, including Mir Alam, a client of Gandhi. When Gandhi and a few Satyagrahis began walking to the registration office, they were followed by the Pathans, who assaulted Gandhi just before he arrived at the office. The Pathans were arrested but Gandhi called for their release, saying he had no desire to prosecute them as they had acted in the belief that what they were doing was the right course.

The injured Gandhi was taken to the nearby home of the Reverend Doke, and he called for the registration official to come to the house to complete the registration process.

Gandhi then went to the Phoenix settlement, which he had established, and wrote various articles, published in the *Indian Opinion*, explaining and justifying his course of action. Although many Indians disagreed with his ideas, they continued to support Gandhi.

However, before long the government reneged on the agreement – a development that some writers say was a result of a misinterpretation of the agreement on the part of Gandhi. The act took account of the voluntary process but retained the compulsory-registration law. Gandhi accused Smuts of 'foul play' and being a heartless man.

On 16 August 1908 thousands of resisters met at the Hamidia Mosque, and more than 2000 registration documents were burnt in a large cauldron. Resisters also began engaging in other forms of resistance - trading without licences, and crossing over from one province to another without permits.

Gandhi spent his time at his office, which became a headquarters for the Satyagraha movement, and also at Phoenix in Natal, where his family were living. He attracted many supporters, especially Christians, who saw his actions as extensions of Christ's principles. Gandhi was close to Oliver Schreiner and her brother, senator and attorney general of the Cape WP Schreiner, and his closest friends included Henry Polak, Hermann Kallenbach and Sonya Schlesin.

The next move in the Satyagrahi's battle saw Sorabji Adajana declare that he would enter the Transvaal without a permit, and present himself for arrest to the border authorities at Volksrust. But Adajana was allowed into the province, and only arrested when he failed to leave. Others who tried to enter the Transvaal were arrested at Volksrust, including Gandhi's son Harilal.

Satyagrahis now became eager to be arrested, and were imprisoned when they tried to cross provincial boundaries. Gandhi was again imprisoned from 10 October to 13 December 1908. He took up cooking duties for his 75 fellow Satyagrahis in prison and performed various laborious tasks, including cleaning toilets.

Gandhi was again imprisoned from 25 February to May in 1909. Smuts sent two religious books for Gandhi, who also read works by Henry David Thoreau, notably the well-known *Civil Disobedience*.

Smuts agreed to keep negotiations going with the passive resisters but secured an undertaking from the imperial government to stop the flow of indentured labourers to Natal – a demand he first made in

1908. By April 1909 the government began to deport some who took part in the campaign.

Throughout the campaign 3000 people were arrested. Fifty-nine people were deported to India in April, and a further 26 in June 1910. Six thousand Indians left the province. Ultimately, the campaign had failed to halt government plans to limit immigration and to secure the general rights of Indian citizens – they were not even recognised as citizens.

Between the two campaigns

Moves were now afoot to forge a Union of South Africa out of the four colonies. Prime Minister General Louis Botha and Smuts went to England to facilitate the process. Gandhi set sail for England and arrived on 10 July 1909, determined to avert anti-Indian legislation that he expected to be enacted in the new union. With the British government acting as mediator, Gandhi and Smuts struggled to reach a compromise. Gandhi demanded equality for the Indians, but Smuts gave little – he was determined to limit Indian immigration, prepared only to allow educated, professional, English-speaking Indians to come to the Transvaal.

Gandhi publicised the Indian issue, meeting with MPs, editors, journalists and various ideologues. He returned to South Africa in November 1909 and in May 1910 established Tolstoy Farm – a retreat for Satyagrahis, a place where their families could live while they were in prison. Kallenbach, who had bought the farm and donated it to the Satyagrahis, taught Gandhi how to make sandals, and the residents engaged in various self-help activities such as farming, carpentry, and making foodstuffs such as bread and marmalade.

The immigration question was at he top of the Union government's agenda, and Smuts was now Minister of the Interior. By 1911 the resistance movement had dwindled and its main activities were negotiations with the government. In 1911 Gandhi met with Smuts and agreed to suspend the campaign.

Towards the end of 1912, Indian nationalist G.K. Gokhale toured South Africa on the invitation of Gandhi, to assess the condition of the Indian community. He travelled from Cape Town to Johannesburg and met with Union cabinet ministers, including their leaders, Smuts and Botha. Gokhale reported to Gandhi that the Black Act and the £3 tax on former indentured labourers would be repealed. Gandhi was sceptical.

In parliament, Smuts said that the £3 tax would not be repealed because Natal's White employers would not allow it. In the Cape colony, a judge ruled that only Christian marriages would be recognised.

Gandhi called for a strike and a renewed passive resistance campaign against the £3 tax at a meeting on 28 April 1913. There were other demands: the right of Indians to travel between provinces, fair trading laws, recognition of marriages conducted under Hindu and Muslim rites, and the right to bring wives and children from India to South Africa.

Gandhi's leadership was not without its detractors. Several critics laid into him, accusing him of egoism, of insincerity – especially since he had not supported earlier campaigns against the £3 tax – and of antagonising the white population.

The 1913 Campaign: Strikers and Marchers

The campaign was launched in September 1913. The first resisters were women who crossed over from the Transvaal into Natal, while women from Natal crossed over into the Transvaal. The Natal women were the first to be arrested, and outraged Indians flocked to join the cause. The Transvaal women were not arrested, so they went to Newcastle and persuaded workers to go on strike.

Gandhi went to Newcastle and spoke to the striking miners, whose employers had turned off the water and lights in their compounds.

On 13 October a meeting was held in Newcastle, and Gandhi was represented by veteran passive resister Thambi Naidoo, who was also president of the Johannesburg Tamil Benefit Society. The meeting formed a passive resistance committee, and Naidoo tried to get workers at the railways to go on strike, but failed. Naidoo was arrested, but was released on 15 October, when the committee addressed 78 workers at the Farleigh colliery. The workers went on strike, were arrested and warned to return to work on 17 October. They refused, and within a week the strikers swelled to 2000. Within two weeks, between 4000 and 5000 workers went on strike. Gandhi, Thambi Naidoo and labour activist CR Naidoo moved around the area, urging workers to join the strike.

On 23 October Gandhi announced that he would lead a march of workers out of the compounds and that they would seek arrest. The plan was to lead more than 2000 strikers across the border into the Transvaal, stopping at Charleston. The march was set to take place from 6 November.

Coalmine owners then sought a meeting with Gandhi, and Gandhi met with them on 25 October at the Durban Chamber of Commerce. Gandhi explained to them that the strike was a response to the government's failure to uphold its promise to Gokhale to repeal the Â£3 tax. The mine owners consulted with government, which denied that they had promised to repeal the tax, and planned to issue an ultimatum for the workers to return to work. On the day, 6 November, before the ultimatum could be communicated, Gandhi led 200 strikers and their families on the march to Charleston. The next day, Thambi Naidoo led a further 300 strikers towards the border. Another column of 250 left the next day, and after a few days some 4000 strikers were on the march for the Transvaal.

The strikers were supported by Indian businessmen, who arranged for food to be distributed along the length of the march. The strike was costing the organisers about Â£250 a day for distributing a minimal diet of bread and sugar. Money was also sent from India to support the strikers.

The strike spread to the south of Natal by the beginning of November, and by the 7th the strike was effectively underway, joined by about 15000 workers in spontaneous fashion. Workers at South African

Refineries, Hulett's Refinery, Chemical Works, Wright's Cement and Pottery Works, and African Boating, among others, joined the strike.

Many strikers congregated in townships and some went to Gandhi's Phoenix settlement. However most, according to Swan, remained in their barracks, refusing to work. Swan also notes that the strikers were unorganised, and motivated by rumour and unconfirmed reports of support from Gokhale, among other reasons.

Meanwhile the marchers were on the move. They went first to Charleston, on the Transvaal-Natal border 60km from Newcastle. They were given 1,5 pounds of bread and some sugar, and told to submit to the police if they were beaten, to behave hygienically and peacefully, and not to resist arrest. They arrived without incident, and were fed with food donated by local businessmen and cooked by Gandhi.

Gandhi informed the government of their intention to continue into the Transvaal, and called on them to arrest the strikers before they arrived, but Smuts calculated that the strike would dissolve before long, and he decided on a policy of non-intervention. Gandhi decided that if the strikers were not arrested, they would march to Tolstoy Farm in Lawley, 35km southwest of Johannesburg, covering 30 to 40km a day.

The marchers then crossed the border into Volksrust, just 2km from Charleston, and proceeded to Palmford, a further 14km away, where Gandhi was arrested. He appeared in court in Volksrust but the judge allowed for bail, which Kallenbach paid, leaving Gandhi free to join the marchers.

When the marchers arrived at Standerton, Gandhi was again arrested, this time by a magistrate. Again he was freed. Two days later, on 9 November, Gandhi was arrested yet again.

On 10 November the government arrested the marchers in Balfour and put them on a train to Natal. Gandhi was arrested on three occasions during the march, and on 11 November he was sentenced nine months' hard labour. Within a few days, Polak and Kallenbach were also arrested and sentenced to three months' imprisonment.

By the end of November, the strike was also coming to an end, and workers began returning to their places of employment.

The strike – by about 20 000 Indian workers in total – paralysed sections of the economy of Natal, especially the sugar industry, and questions arose regarding law and order exercised by the authorities. Rumours that black workers were poised to join the strike sent shivers through the province. Police were sent in and some workers were shot and killed.

The Compromise

Reactions to the strike and march stung the government, especially those of Imperial Britain. Lord Harding, the British viceroy in India, delivered a speech in Madras, India, in which he lashed out at the South African government and demanded a commission of inquiry. The British government also expressed its disapproval, and Lord Harding sent his envoy, Sir Benjamin Robertson, to South Africa to placate local opinion about the Indian question in South Africa.

The government released Gandhi, Kallenbach and Polak on 18 December 1913, and announced the establishment of a commission of inquiry. Gandhi was opposed to the appointment of two of the members of the three-man Soloman commission, but Smuts ignored his objections. Gandhi announced that he would lead a mass march on 1 January 1914, but when white railway workers went on strike, Gandhi withdrew his threat, reasoning that to continue would be against the spirit of Satyagraha.

Smuts and Gandhi entered into a series of meetings to resolve the Indian question – after Smuts had declared martial law while dealing with the railway strike. Acknowledging that Indians saw Smuts as having broken his word after the 1911 negotiation, Smuts insisted that the pair pore over every word so that no misinterpretation was possible. On 30 June, they concluded their agreement, which became law in the form of the Indian Relief Bill.

The agreement gave recognition to Indian marriages, abolished the £3 tax and all arrears accruing from it, set 1920 as the deadline for new Indian immigrants and limited the movement of Indians from one province to another.

Gandhi's detractors launched attacks on him, but Gandhi was satisfied that they had achieved what they had set out to do, and deferred the winning of further freedoms to a later date.

Gandhi left South Africa for England on 18 July 1914, never to return again. However he would continue to have an interest in South African affairs, and would meet with Communist Party leader Yusuf Dadoo years later when the latter went to India to gather support for Indian struggles in South Africa.

The Aftermath in South Africa

Gandhi's struggles didn't culminate in equal rights for South Africa's Indians, who were subject to a string of discriminatory laws in the years after Gandhi's departure from the country in 1914.

In 1946 the Smuts government introduced the 'pegging' and 'ghetto' acts, aimed at limiting the trading and residence rights of Indians, a development that led to a vigorous passive resistance campaign led by Yusuf Dadoo and others.

Chief Albert Luthuli was committed to the principle of non-violence, and led the African National Congress (ANC) until his death in 1967. The ANC was committed to the principle of non-violent resistance until the late 1950s, when it began to contemplate armed struggle. It was the Sharpeville Massacre of 1960 that became the turning point for the ANC, after which violent resistance was sanctioned.

Later, in the 1980s, the UDF also took up the principle of non-violent resistance, especially leaders such as Alan Boesak, Desmond Tutu and Mkhuseli Jack, many of them specifically citing Gandhi as an influence.

International Legacy

Gandhi was admired by African-American leaders in the US from the 1920s onwards, and Marcus Garvey and WEB du Bois publicised his works. A delegation led by Howard Thurman, a Baptist minister, theologian, and academic from the American South, met with Gandhi in 1936. Bayard Rustin and trade unionist A Philip Randolph formed the Congress of Racial Equality (CORE) in Chicago in 1942. CORE staged non-violent protests against racist employment practices in Chicago, and Rustin was jailed for three years when, as a conscientious objector, he refused to serve in the army during WWII.

Gandhi proved to be a major influence on Martin Luther King, who rushed out to buy as many books as he could on Gandhi after listening to a lecture by Mordecai Johnson on non-violent resistance. King and Rustin were the prime movers behind the civil rights movement in the 1950s and 1960s, which reached its height in period from 1963 to 1967.

Gandhi also inspired liberation fighters in Africa, and the Fifth Pan-African Congress, which met in Manchester in 1945, 'endorsed Gandhian passive resistance as the preferred method for resistance to colonialism in Africa'. Kwame Nkruma explicitly cited Gandhi as an influence, and while Kenneth Kaunda and Julius Nyerere never fully accepted the Gandhian philosophy of non-violence, they used the concept to guide their political struggles.

In France, Lanza Del Vasto, who had lived with Gandhi in the 1930s at an ashram in India, founded a Gandhi-inspired organization, the Communities of the Ark. Del Vasto fasted for twenty days in 1957 to end the torture of Algerians by the French military.

The 1980s saw a reawakening of the principle of non-violent struggle, with groups in Poland (the Solidarity movement), Chile, the

Philippines, Palestine (the Intifada movement), China and Burma (Aung San Suu Kyi) adopting Gandhian methods of resistance to oppressive laws.

Other movements also used Gandhian ideas. The Campaign for Nuclear Disarmament cited Gandhi as an influence in its struggle to urge nations to reject the use of nuclear weapons. Environmental movements such as Greenpeace have used non-violence as a method to fight their battles against nuclear proliferation and ecological destruction. The German Green party leader Petra Kelly, an activist against nuclear weapons, has spoken of her admiration for Gandhi, ML King and David Thoreau. She said:

In one particular area of our political work we have been greatly inspired by Mahatma Gandhi. That is in our belief that a lifestyle and method of production which rely on an endless supply of raw materials and which use those raw materials lavishly, also furnish the motive for the violent appropriation of raw materials from other countries. In contrast, a responsible use of raw materials, as part of an ecologically-oriented lifestyle and economy, reduces the risk that policies of violence will be pursued in our name

The Last of The Gandhians in South Africa

Among those who kept the spirit of Mahatma Gandhi alive in South Africa, long after he left the shores of that country in 1914, Nana Sita holds a special place.

Nanabhai, as he was affectionately known, came into prominence during the Indian passive resistance movement of 1946-48 and helped build the alliance with the African majority. He continued non-violent defiance of apartheid until his death in 1969, long after most militants of the liberation movement had become convinced that underground and armed resistance to apartheid had become imperative. Though they disagreed with him, members of the African National Congress and the Indian Congress respected his views and actions - for he continued to defy apartheid, without fear and flinching at no sacrifice.

The regime had been able to supress organized resistance in 1963-64, with the imprisonment and torture of thousands of leaders and activists, and a series of repressive laws. But the adamant defiance of Nanabhai - now old and sick - against forcible racial segregation, was an inspiration to the people. He helped keep alive the flame of peaceful resistance which was to grow in subsequent years.

When he passed away on December 23, 1969, shortly after the centenary of Gandhiji, at the age of 71, the Johannesburg Star wrote that he had enjoyed '*universal respect of South Africans, white and non-white*'. (The Star , weekly edition, December 27, 1969). Sechaba , the organ of the African National Congress, pai tribute to his heroic life, full of sacrifice and devotion to the struggle in which he went to prison seven times. It said:

"*... in paying our tribute to a fallen freedom fighter, the African National Congress works for the day when we can remember publicly in South Africa the man who was our comrade and friend.*" (Sechaba, March 1970).

The life of Nana Sita deserves to be recalled now when the people of South Africa look back at their struggle - armed and non-violent - and acknowledge the contribution made to it by people of varied backgrounds and ideologies, united in uncompromising resistance against racist domination.

Nana Sita was born in Matwadi, a village in Gujarat, India, in 1898, in a family which was active in the Indian freedom movement. He went to South Africa in 1913 and lived for some time with J.P. Vyas in Pretoria, to study book-keeping. Soon after his arrival, Gandhiji, then leading a Satyagraha , went to Pretoria for negotiations with General Smuts and stayed almost two months in the same house.

Identifying himself with the indentured Indian labourers, Gandhiji ate only once a day, wore only a shirt and loincloth, slept on the floor and walked barefoot several miles to the government offices to meet General Smuts. The contact with Gandhiji had a great influence on Nanabhai`s life. He followed the simplicity of Gandhiji, and became a vegetarian, teetotaller and non-smoker. More important, he was always ready to resist injustice and gladly suffer the consequences. He worked for some years in his uncle`s fruit and vegetable business and then started his own business as a retail grocer.

He was active in the religious and social welfare work in the small Indian community in Pretoria. He joined the Transvaal Indian Congress and became secretary of its Pretoria branch. During the Second World War, when the Government imposed new measures to segregate the

Indians and restrict their right to ownership of land - culminating in the Asiatic Land Tenure and Indian Representation Act of 1946 (the *'Ghetto Act'*) - militants in the Transvaal and Natal Indian Congresses, led by Dr. Yusuf M. Dadoo and Dr. G.M. Naicker, advocated mass resistance. They were able to defeat the compromising leaderships of the Congresses and launch a passive resistance campaign in June 1946 with the blessings of Gandhiji. The campaign was directed by the Transvaal and Natal Passive Resistance Councils and over 2,000 people went to jail.

Nana Sita joined the militants as any compromise with evil was against his principles. He became a member of the executives of the Transvaal Indian Congress and the Transvaal Passive Resistance Council. He acted as Chairman when Dr. Dadoo was in prison or on missions abroad. He led a large batch of *'United Nations Day volunteers'* - Indians, Africans and Coloured people - from the Transvaal in October 1946 and was sentenced to 30 days` hard labour. After release, he went to prison a second time. Almost every member of his family - he had seven children - went to jail in the campaign. His daughter - Maniben Sita courted imprisonment twice.

Nanabhai - always wearing the Gandhi cap - became a familiar figure in the Indian movement. His courageous spirit was reflected in his presidential address to the Transvaal Indian Congress in 1948. He said:

"Do we all of us realise the significance, the importance, the heavy responsibility that has been cast upon each and every one of us when we decided to challenge the might of the Union Government with that Grey Steel, General Smuts, at its head? Are we today acting in a manner which can bring credit not only to the quarter million Indians in South Africa but to those four hundred million people now enjoying Dominion Status as the first fruits of their unequal struggle against the greatest Empire of our times?"

"It is for each and every one of us in his or her own way to answer that question with a clear conscience. But let me say that I have nothing but praise for those brave men and women fellow resisters of mine. History has ordained that they should be in the forefront in the great struggle for freedom in this colour-ridden country of eleven million people...Over two thousand men and women have stood by the ideal of Gandhi and have suffered the rigours of South African prison life and they are continuing to make further sacrifices in the cause of our freedom. We at the head of the struggle cannot promise you a bed of roses. The path that lies ahead of us is a dark and difficult one but as

far as I am personally concerned I am prepared to lay down my very life for the cause which I believe to be just." (Passive Resister , Johannesburg, April 30, 1948).

The Indian passive resistance was suspended after the National Party regime came to power in June 1948, but only to be replaced by the united resistance of all the oppressed people.

In June 1952, the African National Congress and the South African Indian Congress jointly launched the *'Campaign of Defiance against Unjust Laws'* in which over 8,000 people of all racial origins were to court imprisonment. Nanabhai was one of the first volunteers in that campaign. He led a batch of resisters which included Walter Sisulu, Secretary-General of the African National Congress. He came out of jail in shattered health.

The next year, when Dr. Dadoo was served with banning orders, Nanabhai was elected President of the Transvaal Indian Congress but he was also soon served with banning orders preventing him from active leadership of the community. Yet, in 1960, during the State of Emergency after the Sharpeville massacre, he was detained for three months without any charges.

With the banning of the African National Congress and the escalation of repression, leaders of the ANC decided to undertake an armed struggle, taking care even then to avoid injury to innocent people. Those who believed in non-violence as a creed or could not join the military wing of the movement faced a serious challenge as even peaceful protests were met with ruthless repression.

Nana Sita - with his Gandhian conviction that resistance to evil is a sacred duty and that there is no defeat for a true satyagrahi - was undeterred. Like Chief Albert Lutuli, the revered President-General of the ANC, he continued to defy apartheid - especially the "Group Areas Act", described as a pillar of apartheid, which enforced racial segregation at enormous cost to the Indian and other oppressed people.

In 1962, Hercules, the section of Pretoria in which Nanabhai lived, was declared a "white area" under the "Group Areas Act". He was ordered to vacate and move from his home - which he had occupied since 1923 - to Laudium, a segregated Indian location eleven miles away. He defied the order and was taken to court on December 10th, the United Nations Human Rights Day.

Denouncing the Group Areas Act as designed to enforce inferiority on the non-white people and cause economic ruination of the Indian community, he told the court overflowing with spectators:

"Sir, from what I have said, I have no hesitation in describing the Group Areas Act as racially discriminatory, cruel, degrading, and inhuman. Being a follower of Mahatma Gandhi's philosophy of Satyagraha , I dare not bow my head to the provisions of the unjust Act. It is my duty to resist injustice and oppression. I have therefore decided to defy the order and am prepared to bear the full brunt of the law.

"It is very significant that I appear before you on this the tenth day of December, to be condemned and sentenced for my stand on conscience. Today is Human Rights Day - the day on which the Universal Declaration of Human Rights was accepted by the world at the United Nations. It is a day on which the people of the world rededicate themselves to the principles of truth, justice and humanity. If my suffering in the cause of these noble principles could arouse the conscience of white South Africa, then I shall not have strived in vain.

"Sir my age is 64. I am suffering with chronic ailments of gout and arthritis but I do not plead in mitigation. On the contrary I plead for a severe or the highest penalty that you are allowed under the Act to impose on me."

He was sentenced to a fine of 100 Rand or three months in prison, and warned that if he failed to comply he would be given twice that sentence. He refused to pay the fine and spent three months in prison. The next year, as he and his wife, Pemi, continued to occupy their home, he was again taken to court and sentenced to six mnonths in prison. The authorities charged him and his wife again in 1965. He appealed to the Supreme Court challenging the validity of the Group Areas Act. The matter dragged on for a year before his appeal was dismissed. When the trial resumed in 1967, Nanabhai read a 19- page statement on the background of the Group Areas Act which he described as a "crime against humanity", and said:

"The Act is cruel, callous, grotesque, abominable, unjust, vicious and humiliating. It brands us as an inferior people in perpetuity, condemns us as uncivilized barbarians... One day the framers of this Act will stand before a much higher authority for the misery and the humiliation they are causing.... If you find me guilty of the offence for which I am standing before you I shall willingly and joyfully suffer whatever sentence you may deem to pass on me as my suffering will be nothing compared to the suffering of my people under the Act. If my suffering in the cause of noble principles of truth, justice and humanity could arouse the conscience of white South Africa then I shall not have strived in vain... I ask for no leniency. I am ready for the sentence."

Many Indians attended the trial and wept when he concluded his statement. He was sentenced again to six months' imprisonment and served the term, declining the alternative of a fine of 200 rand. His wife was given a suspended sentence.

On his release from prison, he said:

"It is immaterial how many other people accept or submit to a law - or if all people accept it. If to my conscience it is unjust, I must oppose it". "The mind is fixed that any injustice must be resisted. So it does not require a special decision each time one is faced with injustice - it is a continuation of one commitment." (Jill Chisholm in Rand Daily Mail , April 6, 1968).

Soon after, on April 8, 1968, Nanabhai and Pemi were forcibly ejected from home and government officials dumped their belongings on the sidewalk. But they returned to the home and Nanabhai never complied with the order until he died in December 1969. Few others followed Nanabhai's example of determined non-violent resistance in the 1960's. The militants among the Indians, espousing armed struggle, had been captured, or went into exile, or tried to rebuild underground structures which had been smashed by the regime in 1963-64.

The traders, who were severely affected by the Group Areas Act, had given up resistance after all their petitions, demonstrations and legal battles had failed. A silence of the graveyard seemed to have descended over the country. But the resistance of Nanabhai was not in vain. It showed that non-violent defiance need not be abandoned even at a time of massive repression or armed confrontation. It inspired people in efforts to overcome frustration and apathy. The Indian Congresses, which had become dormant, were resuscitated in later years and helped build the powerful United Democratic Front.

Nana Sita`s children - Maniben Sita and Ramlal Bhoolia, both veterans of the 1946 passive resistance - played leading roles in the resurgent movement, defying further imprisonment. As the freedom movement recovered, the Soweto massacre of African schoolchildren on June 16, 1976, failed to intimidate the people. Thousands of young people joined the freedom fighters. And many more began to demonstrate their support of the struggle and defy the regime, making several laws inoperative. The struggle entered a new stage.

The mass non-violent defiance campaign, which swelled in recent years like a torrent encompassing hundreds of thousands of people, has made a great contribution, together with the armed struggle and international solidarity action, in forcing the racist regime to seek a peaceful settlement. South Africa, the land where Gandhiji discovered satyagraha, has enriched his philosophy by adapting it under the most difficult conditions.

Nana Sita - who held up the torch when the movement was at an ebb - was in a sense the last of the Gandhians. The mass democratic movement now derives inspiration from many sources, including the experience of the long struggle of the African people and the Gandhian tradition cherished by the Indian community. Nana Sita is remembered with respect as his colleagues in struggle - Nelson Mandela, Walter Sisulu, Ahmed Kathrada and others now out of jail - lead the nation in its continuing efforts to eliminate apartheid and build a non-racial democratic society

Indenture: A new system of slavery?

Was the system of indentured Indian labour "a new system of slavery"?as Hugh Tinker entitles his book? The answer would depend on how the reader defines the word "slavery." In ancient times, for example, under the Romans, a people defeated in war were usually taken over by the conquerors as slaves. The men were imprisoned and assigned to hard labour, where most of them died, while the conquerors absorbed the female population. In more recent times, one tends to think of slavery in terms of the capture of people from West Africa who were taken by slave-traders to America or elsewhere.

These slaves were tied, chained or even yoked to wooden poles and taken against their will to boats where they were herded together like cattle and then transported across the sea. Many never reached the end of the journey where the survivors were auctioned to the highest bidder, and subsequently subjected to the most inhuman treatment, there being no laws to protect them. If the slave married a slave woman, his children were also subject to slavery. Slaves had no rights whatever, and were subjected to merciless punishments and worst of all, could never obtain freedom for himself or for his children unless "set free" by his master.

Both of these descriptions are not applicable to the indentured Indian because he voluntarily contracted his labour for a specific period, and under specific conditions, for example, salary, accommodation, rations and free travel to and from India to the country where the worker was assigned to go.

By Law 14 of 1859 (in addition to subsequent legislation) the British Government introduced labour regulations for employers of Indian labour as well as for employees. While legislation was essentially designed to protect the Indian immigrant, the execution of the law was not always strictly enforced and in the case of Natal, there were employers who defied the law and subjected their employees to a type of Lynch?s law. The Revd W. Pearson who was sent by the Government of India to Natal in 1914 to act as an "observer," was a more impartial critic, but even he commented that "the laws afford him (the indentured Indian), no adequate protection, either in principle or in practice."

Fortunately there emerged one journalist, Henry Polak, who was determined to expose the evils of the system of indenture. In 1903, Polak was a journalist working for the *Transvaal Critic.* He became friendly with Gandhi and, in 1904, became one of the founders of the Phoenix Settlement and subsequently reporter and editor of *Indian Opinion.* In 1906 he was articled under Gandhi and in 1908 qualified as an attorney in the Transvaal Supreme Court. In 1907 he went to India to enlist the support of the Indian Government and on his second visit in 1909, enlisted the support of Mr Gokhale to bring to a conclusion the system of indenture.

Polak became an outspoken critic of the treatment of British Indians in South Africa and in a book entitled *The Indians in South Africa, Helots Within the Empire and How They are Treated,* he exposed the horrors and inhumanity of the system of indenture prior to 1909. Many of the court cases he attended were reported in the press and subsequently, recorded in his book. Unfortunately much of his evidence cannot be substantiated without very detailed search in the archives. On occasions, there are a few incorrect historical details about South Africa in his narratives. As he was one of the few journalists to denounce the system of indenture, his work provides us with a dynamic account of the miseries of the indentured Indian in Natal and, as such, demands our attention:

Discriminatory Attitude

The first aspect which grieved Polak was the discriminatory attitude held by Whites towards Indians. ?Sammy," a common method of addressing an Indian of the labouring classes (said to be an abbreviation of Ramasamy" and similar names), remained very much the second class citizen when it came to travelling on the railway and the tram-cars. He was not permitted to walk on the footpaths (pavement) and the petty arrogance of the lower White officials caused him much irritation, humiliation and bitterness. Hotels did not offer any accommodation for Indians, despite the fact that Indians were rate payers of Durban; they were prohibited from using the municipal baths and the children's paddling pool on the beach.

Recruitment

Polak regarded "famine and want" as the best recruiting agencies. Further, the "ignorant labourer, in penury and starvation" is led to believe before migrating about the "El Dorado tales of South Africa." What does he understand of the contract? What does he know of the laws and social conditions of Natal?

A point on which both Polak and Pearson appear to have been in agreement was the fact that when the labourer was engaged in India, he had no knowledge of the type of work he would do in Natal or who his future employer would be. Certainly after 1895 very few were aware of the £3 annual tax.

Poor Social Conditions

In Natal not only did he encounter new, but poor social conditions of life. These were coupled with the worst aspects of the employment of labour, such as:

. . . "over-long hours of toil, the most arduous drudgery, ill-use, climactic differences, insufficient food supply, temptations to immorality, petty fines and punishments."

The "Coolie marries" were prostitutes and immorality prevailed, partly on account of the non-acceptance of Indian religious marriages and partly through an absence of any social, religious or educational upliftment.

Temporary Slavery

Polak regarded the system as one of "temporary slavery" and totally abhorrent. In fact, the contemptuous attitude of Whites towards Indians could be compared to the Southern States of the USA where the employer treated his servant as,

... "a mere chattel, a machine, a commercial asset to be worked to its fullest capacity, regardless of the human element, careless of the play of human passions. The system lends itself to heartlessness and cruelty, if not on the part of the employers, then on that of his sirdars and overseers."

In his opinion the employers were probably unaware of the hardships they were inflicting on their subordinates, particularly the petty tyrannies, the dehumanising tendencies, the petty prosecutions, the constant injustices and the appalling cruelty which merely contributed to a high rate of suicides. Any breach of contract was regarded as a criminal offence and not a civil matter. In any case, in labour disputes the advantage always lay with the employer. The comparison between the labourer and beast is interesting:

"The Indian labourer is often regarded by his employer as of less account than a good beast, for the latter costs money to replace, whereas the former is a cheap commodity."

Law 25 of 1891 made conditions increasingly difficult for the labourer. Section 25 stated clearly that he could be employed on a Sunday morning up to 8 a.m. "for the care and feeding of animals." However, the law was ambiguous and gave an unscrupulous employer an unfair opportunity to obtain additional labour from his employees. According to Section 26 the employer could be fined up to £2 for failing to observe the clause "up to 8 a.m." On the other hand, if the employee failed to work as requested after 8 a.m., he could be subjected to a fine not exceeding £1.

Section 36 could impose a fine of £5 (half a year's wages) or thirty days imprisonment for "gross insolence, fraud or damage to employer's property." Section 40 stated that the indentured Indian could be transferred to another Estate (subject to the approval of the Protector), a fact which Pearson considered to be "perilously near slavery.? These and many other regulations, provide proof that during the last 25 years of indenture, the labourer had "no adequate protection," and in any case, it became so complicated and tangled in legal jargon, that in most cases, the Law was beyond the reasoning capabilities of an illiterate peasant.

Statistics from the Annual Reports of the Protector for the years 1903 to 1908 reveal that the employers' complaints against their labourers far exceeded the complaints by labourers against employers. Thus, according to Polak, in the first category we find: 5769 labourers were absent without leave or without passes, of these 46 cases were discharged, while 17 were withdrawn; 7767 were absent from roll-call and accused of disobedience, of these 472 cases were discharged while 362 were withdrawn; 1600 labourers left their Estate "in a body;" 135 labourers assaulted their employers; 36 cases were discharged and 362 were withdrawn, making a final total of 15,611 complaints.

As to the complaints by immigrants: 120 lodged complaints against their employers, of which 37 cases were discharged while 42 were withdrawn; 85 managers and sirdars were accused of assault, of which 26 cases were discharged while 42 were withdrawn; finally, 14 employers failed to provide medical attention, 3 cases were discharged and 17 withdrawn, making a final total of 374 complaints.

The reason that the employees' complaints appear so low becomes obvious when the laws relating to "lodging a complaint" are examined.

Lodging a Complaint

According to Section 30, Law 25 of 1891, if a labourer was found to be more than two miles from the place of residence of the employer, without written leave and was on his way to lodge a complaint with the Protector, he could be apprehended and arrested by a policeman or any other higher official. Under Section 31 he could be arrested as a "deserter," unless he could produce a "Pass" or his "Certificate of Discharge." In this instance he could be taken to the Magistrate and fined 10 shillings or serve punishment with hard labour for seven days. For his second offence, he would be punished and serve 14 days, while for a third offence, he would have to serve 30 days. Expenses for his return to his employer would be deducted from the labourer's wages.

If the labourer managed to evade the police and succeed in reaching the Magistrate's offices, he had to convince the Magistrate that his complaint was not "frivolous." If the Magistrate was not satisfied and refused to grant him a pass to proceed to the Protector, the labourer would be fined (and/or punished) and returned to his employer. It must be added that all the days the labourer spent in gaol were ultimately added to his working term before his contract could expire.

If the labourer proceeded directly to the Protector's office, then according to Law 25 of 1891, subsequently amended by Act 17 of 1895, Act 1 of 1900 and Acts 39 and 42 of 1905, and did not have a valid "Pass" to visit the Protector, then the Protector could send him back (under escort) to the Magistrate, where he could be fined (punished) and still be returned to his employer and have to pay all expenses including that of the escort.*

If the Protector accepted the labourer's disposition (for example in a case when his employer had brutally assaulted him), then the labourer "shall be returned to the employer before the complaint is investigated." If there was some irregularity and the Protector was not satisfied, then he could hand the labourer over to the Magistrate, where he could be committed to gaol, fined or punished and returned to the employer.

If the labourer refused to return to his employer, he could be sent by the Protector to the magistrate who would impose the previous punishments.

In cases such as these, Polak regarded the Protector of Indian Immigrants, no longer as his "Protector, but as prosecutor as well as persecutor," and remarks that the Protector becomes the legal advisor of the employer, whilst the poor labourer remains unaided and unrepresented:

"In most cases therefore, if the labourer desired to lodge a complaint against ill-treatment to the Protector and attempted to obtain compensation and redress," he invariably found himself imprisoned and punished "for having dared to seek justice without first obtaining permission."

Polak's condemnation of this system is expressed in very forthright terms:

"This is the most scandalous provision extant on the British Statute-book anywhere. What if these unfortunate wretches have to ask permission to go to the Protector's from the very man they propose to complain against? Is he at all likely to grant it? Indeed, if not, are they to endure on in patience? This section alone is enough to damn the whole Act."

Section 101 of Law 25 of 1891closed the possibilities of a large number of labourers who absented themselves without leave, to complain to the Protector, in which case "they may be brought before any Court and on conviction be punished and fined £2 or imprisonment for two months irrespective of the nature of the complaint."

Polak's conclusions about the Protector and the Magistrate are realistic. He says, "The Protector should be independent," but states that this official very often "becomes the guest of the employer on his tours." As to the Magistrate, he is "born and bred in an atmosphere of semi-slavery and tainted with the Colonial prejudice against and contempt for the Indian labourer." Quite possibly, the Magistrate was a friend of the employer and more likely, even an employer himself. Under these circumstances, "What chance of redress has the complainant?" Further, under these circumstances, would suicide not be the only solution for the unfortunate victim?

By the time the twentieth century came, absconding or desertion, from work had become a major offence and stricter laws were imposed to stop this malpractice. However, as Polak indicates, the law was now so strictly applied that it was almost impossible for the labourer to make a complaint without first being punished for daring to make the complaint)

Despite the fact that Mr Pearson had only been in the Colony for a short period, he diagnosed the malady immediately:

"He (the Protector) makes the assumption, which so many prejudiced Europeans make, that any complaints or evidence put forward by Indians is not to be trusted. He seems to interpret the principles of British justice in a way that assumes all the Indians to be guilty until they are proved to be innocent and all employers of Indians innocent until they are proved to be guilty. And the burden of proof he leaves to the illiterate Coolie whose very language he is unable to understand.?

If we compare reactions by previous Protectors, then it becomes obvious that by 1914 there was complete indifference on the part of the Protector to protect the weak and seek justice. By this time too, as a result of the Government's desire to economise, the Reports of the Protector were no longer published.

Prosecution

Under the existing circumstances, it was a near impossible feat for an employee during the early 1900s to institute civil (sometimes criminal) action against his employer. Fortunately instances did occur where the employers were punished and Polak lists about 20 such cases, with detailed summaries. In all instances, Polak was disappointed at the lenient punishments meted out to the offenders and he comments,

'The penalty is usually quite disproportionate to the offence, whether European or Indian be the accused. But too often it appears that there is one law for the European employer and another for the Indian."

Polak singles out the family of T.B. Robinson of Cato Manor as being of "evil repute" because Robinson senior, his wife, and Robinson junior, were all convicted of offences of ill-treatment against their employees. In the case of Ragavalu (No. 105 396), he had already lost his left hand and had been to the Protector seven times to complain and was eventually rebuked and punished for attempting to commit suicide. Three servants of Sydney Robinson had just served a gaol sentence for refusing to return to work. When they came out, they still refused to return and an infuriated Master Sydney attacked them with a sjambok. The "sympathetic" Magistrate cautioned and discharged Master Sydney, advised the Indians to return to work and commented that, "he knew how aggravating and tantalising they (the Indians) could be!"

In the case of Altsch versus Ginganna, the employer had set his dog upon the labourer. The evidence was clear and Altsch was fined thirty shillings. The Magistrate, commenting on the frequency with which Indians complained against ill-treatment by their masters, said, "This sort of thing must be stopped."

In another case, the Magistrate commented that "if these indentured men had not the protection of the law, their life would not be worth living." This indeed was the case in the so-called Thornville Junction Case, where Messrs Leask, Senior and Junior, were accused of punishing their servants by various means of torture, which included "being cooped up in a box 6 feet by 1 1/2 feet by 1 foot for varying periods" (from one to eight days) without food. Here it was said that the "Coolies live in mortal fear of their masters." The Leasks were subsequently deprived of their labour by the Protector.

In the case of Noyle of Ramsay Collieries, Ladysmith, Devi Singh was so severely assaulted that the Deputy Protector immediately ordered him to hospital. The Magistrate however took a "mild view" and fined the assailant £2-10.

Perhaps one of the most callous instances of inhumanity was when Armitage in a premeditated attack cut off the lobe of the right ear of his servant and thereafter proceeded to dress it. In sentencing Armitage to a £20 fine, the Magistrate remarked.

... "As the Government allowed the cutting of sheep's ears, he (the individual) could not do the same to human being who was placed under his care and protection," and regarded him as a person not fit to have Indians in his charge. Mr Armitage stated that he regarded all indentured Indians as "no better than sheep." As to the people of "evil repute," Polak remarked,

"The Robinsons could not even find it in their hearts to treat their servants as they would expect good cattle. What hope of justice can an indentured Indian expect from such a Magistrate."

A tragic family *case* was that of Ramasamy and Poli who "lived together" (i.e. they were not lawfully married) and had two small children. For some trivial offence, his employer P.D. Simmons "tied him up to a nail in the wall and whipped him until the man's back was one mass of raw and quivering flesh.? That night Ramasamy fled with his family. He reported the incident to the Magistrate, who ordered him to return to his employer, whereupon he went to the Protector, who also ordered him to return to his employer. In the meantime Simmons had reported his servant's desertion and Ramasamy and his family were arrested at the Protector's office. Ramasamy was returned to his employer, but nothing was ever heard again of Poli. Ramasamy could not claim his wife as according to Section 71 of Act 25 of 1891, they were not legally married. This particular case was raised in the House of Commons. Simmons was fined 10 shillings, but the case also aroused deep interest among the Natal press, officials and Colonists.

Another tragic family case was that of Mudaly (No. 116821) and his wife Odda Nagi (No. 116838), who although they were employed as domestic servants, received the rates of pay as for field labourers. His working hours were from 4 a.m. to 9 p.m. with two half hour breaks, while hers were from 6 a.m. to 7 p.m. The elder child was 2 1/2 years old, and all day was tied to a peg in the parent's hut for safety, until the day's work was over. When a second child was born, and a week old, the employer refused to allow the mother to bring the child to work. Fearing the child would starve, the mother gave the child away to foster-parents; the child died of neglect. Complaints to the Protector were of no avail.

According to the terms of indenture, the law prohibited the separation of man and wife and their children. Further, there was no provision for the prevention of separation after allotment. On a particular Estate, Muthialu, the sirdar, paid unusual attention to Valiamma, the lawful wife of Padiachy. When the latter complained about this to his employer, he was thrashed and transferred to another estate, but without his wife. The employer sent Muthialu and Valiamma to the Protector to register their marriage. Three years later after the birth of children, the Protector charged Valiamma for bigamy and in November 1907 fined her £5 which Muthialu willingly paid.

Indentured labourers also had to be very careful when giving any evidence, a factor which has already been emphasised repeatedly, for fear of being accused of perjury and sentenced to imprisonment. Finally, to conclude Polak's list of cases, the author refers again to the couple of "evil repute." T.B. Robinson assaulted Rambally (No. 128349) so severely that for six months thereafter, he was unable to work and was finally shipped back to India as a cripple, leaving his wife and child unprotected. A few days after giving birth to a child, his wife was assaulted by Mrs Robinson.

Polak concludes by quoting statistics for "desertion" under Section 31 of Act 25 of 1891:

Year	No of desertion cases
1901	340
1902	450

1903	520
1904	600
1905	720
1906	850
1907	1100
1908	900

and no doubt succeeded in getting his point across to his reader, namely, the increase in assaults and ill-treatment of labourers was a prime cause of "desertion."

In surveying these examples and statistics given by Polak, the author would like to draw attention to the fact that as approximately 30,000 Indians were still under indenture; Polak's list of aggrieved and battered Indians was a relatively small one. No one will deny that ill-treatment existed, but as to how widespread the evil was cannot be estimated. Polak himself admitted that,

"It is a physical impossibility for the Protector or the estate Medical Officer to completely control abuse on the part of the employers."

The Revd Pearson agreed with the statement, but pinpointed the cause when he wrote:

... "So long as the laws remain as they are, no official can properly protect the indentured Indian labourer."

Medical Treatment

One factor to which the Protector objected was the composition of the later Indian Immigration Trust Board, where the employer majority was 7 to 2 and further, that the Medical Officers were also under the control of the Trust Board. By 1908 the Board was in the hands of the employers and the ideal solution would have been to put the Medical Officers under the control of the State, otherwise remarked the Protector,

... "It appears impossible to me that an Indian Medical Officer can do his duty conscientiously and live in peace with his employers."[119]

Despite the introduction of more and more "Trust" hospitals, the irregularities continued. Polak complained about deduction from the pay of a sick man, and, that when he fell ill, the family only received the rations of one man, and, in some instances, nothing. It was a disgrace to see women working in the fields with babies on their backs, while the fact that there was no employment for women during the winter months, was regarded as inhuman. Extremely sick Indians were usually sent to hospital when there was no longer any hope for recovery while employers were annoyed when cases of illness were reported to the Protector. Polak writes:

"The callousness of some employers and managers is appalling; they look upon their servants as animals and treat them rather worse than such."

Six years later the Revd Pearson commented in similar terms on the "artificial and inhuman relationship between the planter and the indentured labourers," and as he saw the situation,

"Cattle and dogs may be well housed and well fed and even kindly treated as animals, but for men and women we require something more than conditions such as are satisfactory for cattle."

Cases of assault (and consequent injury) to labourers continued to go unreported because the law operated in such a way that the truth was often suppressed and Indians came to the conclusion that they would be safer as "unwilling witnesses."

The Protector was aware that with his reduced powers, he became increasingly powerless to act in the interests of the Indian. After 1900 he complained that he could not afford complete protection to the indentured Indians particularly when they were scattered over thousands of square miles. Referring to the composition of the "Board" he remarked, "It is when the employer domineers over the Indian Medical Officers, that the Indian suffers,? and that such a Board, should in no way "influence the treatment of the indentured Indians in the Colony." Commenting on the high death rate, he stated, "employers continue to be careless and the Indians suffer accordingly."

As "father and mother" to some 30,000 Indians, he was also aware that the number of punishments for trivial offences had increased considerably, and remarked, "a little more sympathy on some estates, and better results would accrue." He even felt that the "won't work" group could be humoured rather than imprisoned.

Like all other aspects of indenture, medical rules also changed constantly. Bill No. AB 74/1909 and Act II of 1910 amended Law 25 of 1891. Henceforth, employers with up to 400 employees paid up to £30 per quarter, i.e., £120 per annum, while those with 400 or more, paid ££ per quarter, i.e., £160 per annum for medical fees to the Trust.

Child Labour

Polak's only reference to child labour was the fact that in the tea factories, young children were working eleven hours per day. However, the Revd Pearson exposed several weaknesses in the system as regards child labour. According to the Protector, although children were "not legally bound to work, in practice they are." This statement summarizes some of the ambiguous regulations that no one appeared able to interpret. The law laid down that "women were to be paid half wages and minors in proportion." Many plantation owners considered that the children were actually under indenture.

This meant a boy's wage could vary from 5 to 9 shillings per month (depending on his age), with an increase of one shilling per month per annum. Thus a boy aged 10 would receive 2 pennies for nine hours work per day. Only a few Estate owners established schools and often children were forced to work, when their parents actually desired them to go to school. In this respect many of the sirdars forcefully took boys away from the schools in order to work on the Estates. The question of rations for women and children was another aspect on which clarity appeared unobtainable.

Female Labour

On some Estates the employers preferred women labour, because they "can be treated with more impunity than the men and do two-thirds as much work." Polak objected to women doing hard manual labour, such as feeding cane-rollers, cutting cane or lifting bundles of cane on to trucks. Apparently this practice existed in other Colonies, and Polak sincerely hoped that "this system of forced labour," on women would be abolished. Generally speaking, the system of indenture was basically evil where the labourers "are completely at the planter's mercy."

Regarding the planter, the system "kills whatever decent instincts he had and turns him into a cruel and remorseless slave-driver, for it is slavery and nothing else."

Repatriation

There are few accounts of indentured Indians being repatriated and still fewer accounts of the return of "wastage" (i.e. unfit workers). Fortunately, M. MacMahon, an ex-planter who sailed on the *Umfuli* on 26 September 1906, was able to provide an account in a Madras newspaper. The *Umfuli*, a vessel of 2300 tons, was packed with 653 passengers whom the writer described as "a disgrace to civilization." The passengers, men, women and children, were "huddled together, without any separation of sexes." Some of them, "were invalids and in a pitiable condition and ought never to have been allowed to leave the hospital." Many were ill with terrible diseases and "the best that was in them having been taken out of them" and quite simply, "they were packed home to die." The writer's final impression was that, "The slavery there (in Natal) under the British flag is indeed worse than the slavery under the Sultan of Zanzibar."

While the Government paid the passage back to India, prospective repatriates from up-country areas such as Newcastle, had to pay their own rail fare to Durban before they were able to join the ship for India. On this point the Protector commented,

... "The law is silent in this connection, but the Board's legal adviser is of the opinion that the Indians have no claim."

In other words, while the rules for emigration from India (e.g. Act XXI of 1883) were implemented, the same law contained inadequate provisions for repatriation.

The Lobito Bay Scandal

On account of deteriorating social conditions in Natal coupled with the fact that so many were unable to pay the £3 annual tax, in addition to a £1 tax per year, many were faced with unemployment, imprisonment and starvation. As a result, when advertisements appeared for the Benguella Railway project in Angola, about 2,250 Indians applied, and were shipped in March 1907. Their contract stated that after service, they would be returned to Natal, free of cost. The experience turned out to be most unfortunate, because according to the *Indian Opinion*, half the labourers died during the first three months in service.

In addition to the non-provision of tents or any other kind of shelter, there was a desperate shortage of water. For months the workers were unable to wash and many succumbed to fever. Living conditions were filthy, there were no medical facilities, and food was scarce. As if this was not enough, when the labourers returned, 948 of them were prohibited from landing in Durban. Relatives and friends in Durban were not given permits to visit them. According to the Government, they were "not domiciled" and would be repatriated "against their will, penniless and friendless back to India without being given the opportunity to prove their domicile."

According to available evidence, the Indian Government broke its rules regarding emigration to non-British countries, because it believed that "the Coolies' interests would be safeguarded." Subsequently it warned the Government of Natal . . . "that both contracts are also open to objection in that they do not make provision for maintenance during sickness or for compensation on account of injuries received."

However, it is doubtful whether the Indian labourers were aware of their legal position as regards their return to Natal, and many, according to the Immigration Restriction Act of 1903, were now prohibited immigrants to Natal. On this episode, Polak writes:

"The Colony of Natal got rid of about 1500 of its Indian population, partly by death, partly by deportation, because the poor wretches could not pay the dead-weight of taxation that was attached to them as the price of freedom," and concludes by remarking that after this fiasco, no more British Indian labourers were assigned to areas outside of British South Africa.

Indian Petitions

In August 1908, at an unprecedented mass meeting of 400 ex-indentured Indians, the petitioners:

... "strongly urge the stoppage of indentured Indian immigration to Natal, under the present state of the law, which reduces indentured labour to a form of slavery."

They complained about the callous attitude of their employers who,

... "are content to regard the Indian labourer as a machine, from which the last ounce of work is to be ruthlessly extracted, and which may then be "scrapped" with other outworn instruments of labour," and remarked that when they were indentured, they were not acquainted with the laws of the country and with the terms of their agreement.

Further,

... "Neither were they aware of the hardships and disabilities they would have to undergo here as indentured or free Indians."

In fact,

... "their position under indenture was so miserable and the necessities of life here are so dear, that your petitioners are virtually unable to save any sum in order to enable them to go back to their country after the expiry of their indenture, or to pay the £3 tax, should they choose to remain in this Colony after giving the best years of their lives under indenture.?

Owing to the vigorous enforcement of the Act, they now faced "intolerable difficulties" which, in some instances, made law-abiding citizens turn to crime. They regarded the enforcement of this iniquitous measure (the £3 tax) on women as :

"unprecedented and contrary to the principles of justice and quite repugnant to the British idea of freedom and liberty."

In one notorious case, a woman in Stanger was imprisoned and her hair shaved off because she could not pay the £3 tax. Polak reported that since that incident, the Natal Government gave instructions that no female Indian prisoner could be subjected to such treatment except on the specific instruction of the prison Medical Officer.

In September 1908, the Natal Indian Women's Association also forwarded a petition on the disastrous effects of the £3 tax on family life. The Act was responsible for breaking up homes, alienating the affection of husband and wife, and, in many instances, separating mother and child. Men who could not find employment were deserting their families and as a result many women were forced into immoral living. The complaint was that £3 was the price for freedom or constant imprisonment, and the fact that:

"There is no precedent in the legislation of any other country under the British flag where women are taxed for the privilege of living with their husbands or under the protection of their natural guardians."

The author has chosen this particular statement by Henry Polak to illustrate that on many occasions throughout his writings, one is under the impression that he has taken the credit for a fact which could be attributed to another source. In the case of the latter statement, there is remarkable similarity to the wording from the Women's Association letter, signed by Miss C.R. Sigamoney (Hon. Secretary) which reads:

"The Law is an unprecedented one in the history of the world and it is repugnant to British justice to impose a tax upon women and girls to live with their husbands or natural guardians." Unfortunately the date on the archival document is illegible.

Forced Re-indenture

Under Act 42 of 1905, Indians could gain the right of a free return passage to India, if they **re-**indentured for a further two-year period. As a result of the iniquities of the £3 tax, many were forced to re-indenture. For example, in 1908, out of 7 735 who had served their five-year term, 3 304 re-indentured (i.e., 43 per cent) about 50 per cent returned to India while the rest became "free." Thus we see that only a very small percentage could "afford " to pay the £3 tax.

Under the five-year plan, it was impossible for the average indentured Indian to save any money. Polak estimated that under the average five-year period, savings had declined from £1 6-7-6 in 1904 to £5-5-2 it 1907. Previously under a ten to eleven year stay, it was possible to save a considerable amount, especially during the time one was free. The Protector of Indian Emigrants in India estimated that while average annual savings in 1907 in Mauritius was about £4-18-2, and in Jamaica about £4-14-8, in Natal it was among the lowest at £1-1-2.144.

Another contributory factor was that although under Act 17 of 1895 the wages for re-indentured Indian was stipulated to be 16 to 20 shillings per month for each succeeding year of service, in reality man3 employers paid only between 10 and 14 shillings.

Discontinue Indenture

Polak questions the wisdom of a man returning to India after five years with £8 or less in his pocket. "Is it not inhuman to repatriate them after having made Natal habitable and productive?" he asks and question further,

. . . "What is it but taking the best of our servants and then refusing them the enjoyment of their reward', Forcing them back when their best days have been spent for our benefit"?

Polak criticises Natal's immigration policy when he says that,

"Natal while closing the front door upon Asiatic immigration, opens the back door for its further artificial introduction, contrary to the wishes of the Indian community," referring to the different attitudes held in Natal towards "free-passenger" and "indentured" immigrants. In short, there was only one way to rectify the evil, and that was to stop indenture altogether.

By 1908 the possibility of a future union of the four British Colonies of Southern Africa had become reality. The other South African Colonies, alarmed at the continued increase in the numbers of indentures Indian immigrants to Natal, subtly urged Natal to discontinue the system of indentured labour. The Natal Governor, Sir Mathew Nathan, was well aware of the intricate situation. For example, when commenting on the three controversial Bills of 1908 stated that if these Bills which concerned the merchant class were passed, they would- ultimately have "an evil effect on the whole body of Indian subjects of the King," and wisely forecast a near impossible solution:

"Repatriation ... is the only solution which would be completely satisfactory to the white races in the sub -continent."

After Union it was the National Party under Dr Hertzog which relentlessly pursued this theme at the Cape Town Conference (1926-7), and at the Second Cape Town Conference (1932). Finally in 1960, exactly a hundred years after the arrival of the first Indians, the South African Government finally accepted, rather reluctantly, that the Indians were citizens of the Union of South Africa.

By the time of Union there was also popular agitation throughout Natal for the abolition of the system of indenture. The newspaper, *Indian Opinion,* by highlighting cases of ill-treatment, merely stirred up public opinion particularly amongst the Indians. Polak contributed much in this respect, while Albert West considered the system to be "unjustifiable and inhuman" and attacked the system in principle. Slavery in any form, whether it was partial, temporary or indenture, remained objectionable on humanitarian grounds. The historian, Pachai, concludes very aptly when he says:

"If the labourer was accepted in Natal with half the alacrity and affection as was his labour, the operation of the indenture system in the Colony might have conformed more closely to the ethics of human conduct."151

The reluctance on the part of the British Government to discontinue indenture must also be considered as a contributory factor because,

"It took a long time before either the Indian or the Colonial authorities would admit that most of those who returned (to India) had obtained little benefit from their exile."

Community of Indians

Indian passive resistance in South Africa: 1946 – 1948

2010 marks 150th anniversary of the arrival of the Indian indentured workers and the birth of this community in South Africa. Durban is home to the largest Indian population in South Africa. They contribute to the multicultural atmosphere of the city and many Indian rituals and traditions can still be observed today.

Indenture and Freedom

Between November 1860 and 1911 (when the system of indentured labour was stopped) nearly 152 184 indentured workers from across India arrived in Durban. But in 1885, in order to maintain the labour, a 3 pound tax was implemented on formerly indentured Indians who failed to reindenture or return to India after completing their contracts. By 1910, nearly 26.85% indentured men returned to India, but most chose to stay and thus constituted the forbearers of the majority of present-day South African Indians.

After completing their indenture, many rented land to grow fruit and vegetables for the local market. In 1885, the Wragg-Commission noted that Indians dominated the food produce market.

Those who did not turn to the food market, became entrepreneurs and opened stores and hotels, while others made a living through gardening, hawking and fishing. In order to force Indians into employment, the government introduced in 1910, a 3 pound tax on all non indentured adults, boys under 16 and girls under 12 and older. Many workers were forced to reindenture to avoid tax. By 1913, approximately two-thirds of workers were on second and third contracts. In 1914, this tax was abolished after the Passive Resistance Campaign of 1913.

Passenger Indians

Indian culture and way of life necessitated commodities such as payer goods, spices, cooking utensils, religious books and clothing. This is where the Passenger Indians came in and fulfilled the need for traders. This group who were mainly Gujerati speaking, but included a stronger contingent from South India, were able to maintain links with India through travel and visits to home villages. The first Indian shop which sold condiments and other delicacies was opened in Field Street by Bauboo Naidoo.

In 1875, the first 'Arab' store was opened in West Street by Aboobaker Amod, a Memon trader from Porbander. Muslims refereed to themselves as 'Arab' to distinguish themselves from other Indians. About two decades after Indians settled here, the Wagg Commission observed that the anti-Indian sentiment was driven by White traders, farmers and workers who feared agricultural competition.

In addition, the Pietermaritzburg Chamber of Commerce noted a growing fear from White settlers and their demand for all Indian traders to be lawfully required to produce identity documents with a photograph on demand. Despite all this, the Indian trader prospered, much to the disappointment of the White settlers.

Many Indian traders became successful by trading with the local Black population in the remote areas by selling items in small quantities and giving items on credit. Often their goods were cheaper than their White counterparts. This made the White traders very envious and prompted them to influence the government to pass numerous laws that would restrict the Indian trader's right to a living and trade.

However, the government failed in its attempts to destroy the Indian trader.

Areas of Settlement

Indentured labourers had to be given accommodation by their employers; however, they had to find their own way after indenture. Those who turned to agriculture usually stayed on the land which they were renting.

The railways as well as the Municipality erected barracks for their Indian labourers. Similar constructions were erected by other employers throughout the Durban area. But due to the shortage of housing, these and similar constructions became overcrowded and soon turned into slums. In the central town area, merchant class Muslims settled in a racially exclusive central district of Durban. Some traders lived in their shops while others rented flats just above their businesses. Later these also became overcrowded. Meanwhile the citizens of Durban were not happy with the arrival of the Indians in the town areas. They regarded this as an unwarranted intrusion upon the colonial atmosphere.

The government realised that the housing problem had to be solved and thus set aside several locations for Indians in areas around Natal.

But living conditions in these areas were poor as families lived in cramped yards, sharing a communal toilet.

The main areas that Indians occupied were beyond the Umgeni River, in Riverside and Prospect Hall and further inland at Duikerfontein and Sea Cow Lake. Springfield and Sydenham were also predominantly Indian. Indians also settled in areas such as Mayville, Cato Manor, Clairwood and Magazine Barracks, and the Bluff.

Even though informal segregation existed at this time, it was not until 1922 that the first major restriction came about when the municipality reserved the right to exclude Indians from purchasing any municipal land.

The Slums Act was passed in 1934 in order improve conditions and to facilitate 'slum clearance' in the city. In actual fact the Act meant the expropriation of Indian property. One of the main ideas behind this being city cleanup and industrial expansion. However, as late as the 1970's Indians in places like Tin Town in Springfield still lived in shacks without basic services.

By 1936, only 20% of Indians owned houses in Durban that were made of brick, stone or concrete, the rest lived in wood and iron structures. The government did not provide electricity as they did not trust that the Indians could handle it.

In the 1940's the Pegging Acts of 1942 – 43 and the Ghetto Act of 1946 were passed. This act gave the government the right to remove and destroy shacks and homes in some areas under the pretext of improving unsanitary living conditions. In the 1940's measures to contain the aforementioned 'Indian penetration' became a major focus of Indian community activism (**see** Passive Resistance Campaign 1946).

The Ghetto Act paved the way for the Group Areas Act passed in 1950, which proclaimed certain areas White. This meant that the non-White communities who found themselves in these areas would have to be moved to other areas designated as 'Indian', 'Coloured' or 'African'. Therefore, Indian residents in Durban, like all non-White South Africans, were segregated by race.

This caused a major uproar and led to the two year passive resistance campaign from 1946 to 1948 when several thousand Indians courted arrest. Despite the protests, the act was passed in 1948. The Group Areas Act formalised the process.

By 1950, the Group Areas Act was created by the apartheid government. This act displaced thousands of Indians and Africans from their homes and businesses.

Indians were removed from areas such as Mayvile, Cato Manor, Clairwood and Magazine Barracks, and the Bluff. By 1950 there were adverts in the newspapers for an exclusively Indian suburb called 'Umhlatuzana'. Later, Red Hill and Silverglen (later Chatsworth) were also advertised. Reservoir Hills, which was also declared an Indian area was able for the more well to do Indians. In the north of Durban, La Mercy and Isipingo Beach were also designated Indian areas. In Merebank, purpose built houses replaced the poor settlements and by the late 1950's a reconstructed Merebank offered cheap houses for which the purchaser had ten years to pay.

Planned in 1960 the largest designated Indian area, Chatsworth, opened in 1964. It consisted of eleven neighbourhood units containing 7000 sub-economic and 14 000 economic houses. It was deliberately built to act as buffer between the White residential areas and the large African township of Umlazi in Durban.

In Mount Edgecombe, indentured migrants occupied tent-like homes near the temple and workers were housed on the sugar mill. Some of the structures had existed for more than a hundred years before the newer structure near Campbells Town and the surrounding areas came about.

The community at Mount Edgecombe was a poor one where entertainment was an important part of daily life. However, with the introduction of upmarket estates, the fortunes of people living there today are very different to what they were many years ago.

Today, the majority of Indians still live in these areas.

Education

Indians were regarded by the British as a 'temporary investment", thus, for almost a decade, they made no educational provisions for workers of their children.

Workers quickly realised that being educated in their mother tongue was not enough to succeed in South Africa, while many employers were under the mistaken notion that many of them were illiterate.

The missionaries were the first to establish schools for Indians. The first school, erected by the Roman Catholic Church in 1867, housed 30 pupils. By 1883, 21 mission schools were established in Natal. Parents also made efforts to teach their children their mother tongue.

In 1896, the first government recognised Indian school offering lessons in English was opened. A government grant was made available to Rev Ralph Stott to run a day school for children of plantation Indians.

Evening classes were held for older pupils but both schools catered only for boys.

Up to 1894, the children of Indians with 'European habits' were admitted to the Government Model School in Durban.

In 1878, government began to involve itself in Indian education and by 1885, there were 24 state-aided schools for Indians. By 1889, the admission of male pupils to European schools ceased, girls, however were allowed to attend until 1905.

By 1909, there were 35 Indian schools, 31 of which were government-aided. In the same year, an Education Commission recommended that it should be made compulsory for the holder of any estate where there were 20 or more children of indentured workers between five and twelve years of age to provide basic education, using teachers of their own nationality.

1927, was a significant turning point for Indians in South Africa as Cape Town Agreement was concluded between South Africa and India. By then only a third of Indian children were attending school. Although, there was an increase in enrolment, most schools were 'aided' and parents had to raise funds to pay towards the cost of the building.

Unemployment and poverty

During the inter-war years unemployment and low pay resulted in larger scale poverty amongst the Indians. The situation was the result of White labour policy which saw a drop in Indian employment in industry and was exacerbated by the depression. Extensive poverty became a pervasive feature in Indian life in Durban during the 1930's and 1940's. Diseases like T.B and bronchial asthma manifested due to extreme poverty. In places like Cato Manor, the clay soil and cement floors caused rheumatism, arthritis and chest infections. Dysentery, diarrhoea and pneumonia were also present due to poor diet, defective sanitation, overcrowding and lack of ventilation.

Family, religion and language

Sport, welfare, educational organisations, family and religion all formed a crucial part in racial and ethnic identity amongst the Indians in Durban. The apartheid system allowed the Indians to rebuild aspects of their social and economic life with the minimum outside influence.

They created a new life for themselves that was not based on the one they left behind in India as culture was modified by new occupations and circumstances which changed their needs.

Family membership was the most crucial element in Durban. The extended family household was very common with brothers, their wives and children living in a common household with the father of the men as patriarch.

Marriage across race, language and religious lines were rare, even marriages across religious lines caused great unhappiness amongst the groups. In the early years, Indians considered marriage within the group as extremely important for maintaining group identity. This tradition is slowly dying out as inter-religious and even inter-racial marriages are becoming more common.

Women played a crucial role in the construction of social and economic life in Durban. The mother was and still is pivotal.

The extended family was an essential means of surviving in the urban milieu and should not be seen as a force because of tradition brought from India. Social and economic responsibilities were clearly demarcated in the household and resources were pooled in a common family budget. This system allowed many families to escape the extreme poverty. Income pooling and co-residence all contributed to the family cohesion.

Males had greater access to education and jobs, were more involved in sports, community and political organisations and had greater freedom of movement.

Closeness was maintained with cultural heritage which was reinforced by ethnic and racial clustering. The family promoted and strengthened ethnic identity and emphasized community-minded ethic.

Religion

The majority of Indians that live in Durban are Hindus. In 1936, there were 79, 64% Hindus compared to the 14, 74% Muslims and a small percentage were Christian.

The Hindus in Natal were mainly Sanatharist which is more popular and less scripturally orientated. They place strong emphasis on the myths, legends and vibrant stories which abound in ancient Hindu epic scriptures. Religious culture affected every aspect of life and because it was part of folk tradition in all parts of India, local Hindus were able to transcend regional, cultural and linguistic differences.

Mosques and Temples

The building of mosques and temples in Natal was an important step in reconstructing religious life and these became a community centre.

The building of temples became a community effort and was considered a sacred act. Initially, Indians erected tiny wattle and daub thatch shrines and temples on sugar cane estates. The earliest temples include those at Umbilo (1869), Mount Edgecombe (1875), Newlands (1896), Cato Manor (1882), Ispingo Rail (1870) and Sea View (1910). In 1869, the first wood and iron temple was built in Rossburgh near Clairwood. The tradition of building temples whenever a community was formed was continued by Free Indians. The building of temples was a major achievement for the Indians given their poverty, arduous work and confinement to specific plantations. The temples not only helped preserve religion but became a source of security for many. It was here that communal worship was experienced, communal births, marriages and death ceremonies were observed and festivals carried out.

The mosque which was also a means to building community spirit became the centre of Muslim worship and congregational prayer. The first mosque was built in 1881 in Grey Street by passenger Indians, Aboobaker Jhavery and Hajee Mohamed Dada. It is the largest mosque in the southern hemisphere. The second mosque was built in 1885 by Ahmed Tilly and Hoosen Meeran in West Street.

In an effort to teach Islam to adults and children alike, Mohamed Ebrahim Soofie established mosques and madrasahs all over Durban. Born in Bombay, Soofie who arrived in Durban in 1895, displayed mystic tendencies and was very interested in Sufism. Soofie built mosques and madrasahs in Riverside (1896), Springfield (1904), Westville (1904), Overport (1905), Sherwood (1905), and Sea Cow Lake (1906). At the time of his death in 1910, Soofie had built a total of 13 mosques.

Muslim children still attend madrasahs and many of the original schools are still continuing today. There are also many other private smaller madrasahs that have spring up all around Durban to accommodate children living now in areas that was previously reserved for "Whites only."

Visits from missionaries from India increased knowledge and awareness amongst Indians in South Africa. Bodies were established to unite Hindus and impose common practices and festivals. These religious bodies provided direction in the fields of vernacular education and religious training. In 1906, Professor Bhai Parmanand formed the Hindu Young Men's Society and encouraged members to study Tamil, to engage in missionary work and to visit India in order to understand their cultural heritage. Swami Shankeranand followed in

1908 and established Hindu societies in Sydenham, Mayville and Sea Cow Lake. Swami Shankeranand encouraged Hindus to circulate money amongst them in order to establish educational institutions, political bodies and co-operative movements.

In order to unite Hindu market gardeners, he established the Indian Farmer' Association. The Swami, who was conservative, was determined to forge a strong environment through conciliation with the white authorities that were favourable to the teaching of Hindu religion, culture and language. In 1909, he got the Durban Veda Dharma Sabha to choose the licensing officer to present an address to the retiring Governor of Natal. Many were not happy with this as Indians were experiencing licensing problems and this gesture would indicate that all was well in this area. When King Edward died in May 1910, the Swami called on all Hindus to observe mourning. He also tried to organise a sports and festivities day to mark the coronation of the new King and he obtained leave for indentured Indians to attend funeral services. He was opposed to Gandhi and his passive resistance efforts as he believed that the authorities were prejudiced against such actions.

In 1912, the Swami organised a conference to systematize Hinduism, which led to the formation of the Hindu Maha Sabha. The objective of this organisation was to promote friendship and unity amongst Hindus, to improve general knowledge through reading, encourage the growth of Hindi, and to create a love for the motherland and assist the needy. Through his untiring efforts, the Swami increased religious awareness.

Between 1905 and 1915, 12 Hindu organisations emerged due to the efforts of visiting scholars. The Gandhi-Tagore Lectureship Trust, established in 1946, aimed to bring out a lecturer every year to educate Indians in Natal on culture, philosophy, ethics and civilisation.

In 1946, The Maha Sabha designed a flag which is still used at temples, schools and private homes.

Religious education and drama

Hinduism was mainly taught at home while temples served as a source of community bonding. The religion was initially taught by parents while elders recited mythological stories from Indian literature to the young or told religious stories orally. From the early 1900's, books on prayers, histories of divine saints and places and praise poems were sold by Moothoosamy Bros in Grey Street. In 1931, VMM Archary wrote the "Thotra Malai" which contained sixteen short prayers that were sung at different times of the day. Hindus performed "pujas" which is a prayer performed by a pandit (priest) for every significant event, a tradition which still continues today. Prayer flags called " jhandi" are raised in front of the house. These were made from bamboo poles which flew a red pennant and it remaines there until the next puja is performed. The jhandi makes it easy to recognise a Hindu home in the area.

Other ceremonies include the Katha readings which are stories and songs with a religious point that are read by a priest to mark an important occasion or to fulfil some vow. Satsangs (readings and songs from scriptures) and Yagnas, which were intricate and costly sets of rites and sermons, were also held.

A room is generally set aside for devotional prayer with the mother lightening the God lamp at sunset and sunrise for the whole family to pray. This nurtured a collective feeling and a common cause of worship.

Muslims received formal education from a very young age at madrasahs, which were in the early days, usually attached to the mosques. One of the earliest madrasahs was the Anjuman Islam School which was opened in 1909 and attached to the West Street Mosque. Similarly, the May Street Mosque also had a madrasah attached to it in 1920. The Hajee Ahmed Mohammed Lockhat Wakuff

(Trust) established in 1922 by AM Lockhat established a number of madrasahs around the Durban area, many of them still exist today. During the 1940's and 1950's, leaders like AI Kajee aand MM Moola attempted to combine religious and secular education by building schools such as South Coast Madrasah State Aided School, the Ahmedia State Aided Indian School, Anjuman Islam State Aided School and Orient Islamic High School.

Festivals

Mohurram

According to Goolam Vahed, Indian festivals and rituals are very visible markers of racial and ethnic identity and strengthen the links between individuals and the communities in which they live. The major Muslim festival called Mohurram is held on the tenth day of Mohurram, which is a month in the Islamic calendar. This festival is held to commemorate the martyrdom of Imam Hussein (the grandson of the Prophet Muhammed PBUH) who was killed on this day in battle. In the early days, Hindus even participated in this festival as there was a great feeling of unity amongst the Indian community.

During the early 1900's, preparations for the festival began two weeks before the actual day. Bamboo and other materials were collected to build a tajjia, a miniature mausoleum constructed in wood and covered in coloured paper with gold and silver tinsel. The mausoleum, which was between 15 to 25 feet in height, consisted of three levels, each, rising from within the other. The craft of building tajjias was passed on from generation to generation and undertaken with great care and pride. Each area attempted to build the most attractive tajjia.

On the tenth day of Mohurram, people gathered around each tajjia, pulled it by hand while singing songs in memory of Hussan and beating on drums or carrying out stick fights. The chariots were led by dancers who painted their faces and bodies as *"tigers who were supposed to prevent the corpses of slain martyrs from being crushed at the battle where Hussan was killed"* (Vahed, p192). The tigers were excellent wrestlers and later during the day, the wrestlers from the different districts would compete against each other to determine who the best wrestler was.

The tajjias were usually dumped into a river or the sea. Although this practice continues to be a feature in some of the communities, it is slowly fading out. The festival of Mohurram provides an opportunity for expressing local community and neighbourhood identity. It united families and neighbourhoods.

Although this festival is not so widely practised today, there are communities like the Clairwood community which still carry out the rituals on a yearly basis.

Kavadi

Kavady is celebrated in February and May each year in honour of God Muruga, who Hindus believe has the power to cure people of their illnesses and gets ride of misfortune. Those who have been afflicted with disease or sickness, fast, pray and use kavady as a means of penance. Some participants stick needles and pins in their tongues and cheeks, or draw chariots with strings knotted into large hooks protruding from the fleshy parts of their bodies. The procession which started from the river bank ended at the temple.

The Kavady is made from a bamboo which is bent into an arch and decorated with marigolds, ferns, palm shoots, peacock feathers and coconuts. A brass container filled with milk is attached to each corner which the devotee uses to wash the statuette of the deity. Thousands attend the Kavady festival in order to be blessed by participants. In the early days, people travelled long distances to the temples with clothing and utensils and stayed there for several days until the festival was over. This also strengthened the link between the individual and the community. The Kavady festival is still a very strong part of Hindu tradition which continues today.

Mariamman

The Mariamman (commonly known as porridge prayers) is a festival associated with the Goddess who is believed to be the cause and cure of various infectious diseases including smallpox and measles. During this festival, devotees offer *"cool foods"* (Vahed, p197) such as milk porridge, pumpkin and coconut to the Goddess to cool her anger. The food which is placed in a bucket around the temple is eaten by the devotees. A chicken or goat is usually sacrificed and the blood spilt on the earth to represent life and fertility. This festival which is celebrated on Good Friday is attended by many.

Draupadi (firewalking)

The Draupadi festival, commonly known as firewalking, is celebrated annually in March, in honour of the Goddess Draupadi who is regarded by Hindus as *"the model of duty, love and devotion and who bore various trails with great fortitude"* (Vahed, p198). According to South Indian tradition, the Goddess walked on fire in order to cleanse herself from attempts to degrade her. The ceremony involves devotees, called 'Soutris', walking through a ten metre fire pit and those who have faith in the Goddess believe that she walks the coals before them and cools it. Devotees bless the crowd by placing holy ash on their foreheads.

Diwali

The festival of Diwali is the most celebrated amongst the Hindu communities both in Durban and around South Africa. Known as the 'festival of lights," it is celebrated at the end of the autumn harvest in India with ceremonial worship of the Goddess of wealth and learning.

Language

The retention of the vernacular language was an important concern for Indians during the 1930's and 1940's. The Hindu Maha Sabha which was formed in 1912 encouraged the growth of Hindi. In 1925, the Arya Pratinidhi Sabha was formed to promote art, culture and civilization of India and to promote the study of Indian languages. From 1936, free vernacular classes for adults was organised by the Vedic Educational Society. By 1945, the Sabha had 29 affiliate institutions that followed a uniform syllabus. The Tamil, Gujerati and Telegu communities also formed similar organisations to teach the vernacular.

The vernacular schools which were run between 3pm and 5pm taught grammar, singing and provided general religious knowledge. Not many of these exist today and much of the language has been lost as the majority of younger generation Indians cannot speak their vernacular language. English has become the language in most Indian homes in Durban.

From the 1920's and 1930's, Hindi music record and sound films played a significant role in Indian life in Durban. The cinema became a regular feature for many Indians living in Durban. There were five or 6 theatres in central Durban, one in Mayville and one in Jacobs. People often travelled great distances to see these movies. The theatres were Indian owned, particularly by the Moosa and Rawat families. The films had a positive impact for the language retention and became a source of religious education fro many Indians South Africans. Today Indian movies are still widely watched by young and old alike although most have English subtitles. Cinemas like the one at Suncoast regularly screen Indian movies to cater for the huge Indian population in Durban.

The films made accessible a large number of songs which became important in cultivating Indian language. Stores like Roopanand

Brothers and Orient Saloon opened where people could purchase the songs.

Indians in South Africa could not get by with vernacular only as a result of language difference amongst them and it should be remembered that they operated in a colonial urban milieu where they had to communicate with others who spoke other languages. Initially, they used Fanagalo, a mixture of Zulu, English and Afrikaans but over time a distinct South African English became the main language of communication between Indians. The vernacular remained the language of the home for most until the 1960's, thereafter, English became the main language and by 1990, 97,5% of Indians regarded it as their first language.

Cuisine

Durban is famous for its 'bunny chow'. This popular takeaway, which is a bread and curry dish, is made by hollowing out the centre portion of the bread, filling it with curry and then capping it with the portion that was cut out. There are many stories as to how, when and where the popular takeaway originated. One story is that originated in a 'Bania' (a name used for the Gujerati speaking people) restaurant, in Grey Street, Durban. Another story states that migrant workers needed to hold their vegetable curries in a form of container and resorted to using their bread to hold their lunch together.

But whatever the story, a trip to Durban will not be the same without trying the 'bunny chow.'

The Indians in Durban have and still contribute greatly towards the growth of this Province. Their festivals, temples, mosques and culture continue to be a great tourist attraction for this city

Social Customs

Many Indians living in South Africa still maintain their ancient traditions and customs with the unique Indian cuisine being a firm favourite among South Africans. Indians both Muslim and Hindu stay in South Africa, but the first group of Indians to set foot on African soil consisted mainly of Hindus. They brought with them their ancient caste system and laws, a laid out social hierarchy which governed everything from your type of work to the marriage partner you would be expected to take. However the caste system was soon abandoned by Indians in their new found home leaving economic status and intellectual achievement to develop as the new yardstick for admission to social acclaim. Hinduism is not solely a religion but also a life philosophy which accepts the existence of many different gods and deities. The head god, Brahma, Vishnu and the god of destruction Shiva are some of these. Hindus also believe in the concept of reincarnation or many rebirths and most have private household altars where offerings can be made and prayers be said. Weddings continue to appear as prominent highlights on most Indians' social calendars. In the past, the bride was expected to live with her husband in his parental home. However, now days in the modern Indian community the emphasis has shifted from the extended family to that of the nuclear family. But also changing with the times has been the role of women, with more and more Indian women becoming educated and economically active.

Sampson Jeremiah

Community of Indian in Lenasia

From the very beginning, settlement in Lenasia was a contentious issue, driven with debates about race, class, collaboration with and resistance to apartheid. Calls were made by the Indian Congress to reject the plans of the newly elected Nationalist government, but the drastic shortage of housing for Indians in areas close to the Johannesburg city centre meant that some, especially the very poor workers, welcomed the offer of a place to stay and conditions which, although minimal, were a vast improvement on their previous lot.

After the National Party won the 1948 election on an apartheid ticket, the government moved speedily to introduce new laws and to implement these. The existence of suburbs like Sophiatown, where people of all races, including poorer White people, mixed more or less freely, had always irked those who wanted to see segregation more rigorously effected. This tendency, now ensconced as the ruling party, suddenly had the power to realise these plans – to unscramble racial mixing, separate the groups and deposit them in racially exclusive locations. The first step was the passing of the Group Areas Act in 1950.

Indians had been living in various suburbs in and around Johannesburg, in varying numbers, for decades. In towns such as Turffontein little pockets forming small communities had taken root, while in others there were larger communities, such as in Fordsburg, Doornfontein, Vrededorp, Sophiatown, Newclare and other areas.

The Nats at first proposed an alternative to re-housing the Indians by offering them a free passage back to India, but very few took up this offer. So the plan was for the Indians to be moved to a suburb populated only by Indians. The government at first offered the community the area today known as Robertsham, about 10km from the city, but community leaders refused to be housed there. Eventually some accepted relocation to an area known as Lenz, despite the fact that the Indian Congress had rejected the Group Areas Act.

Mahommed Jajbhay, Rev Sigamoney, Mahommed Abed, Ebrahim Dadabhai and Advocate Minty formed the Transvaal Indian Organisation, which was tasked to persuade Indians to move to Lenz.

Indians living in Sophiatown were the first to move to Lenz as housing had been the biggest issue for all the people living there. Entire families lived in tiny rooms because space was in such short supply. Rents were extremely high, and to secure living space tenants were also required to pay other costs, such as goodwill, a sum to guarantee the right to rent the lodgings in the first place.

Working class people in areas such as Sophiatown and Newlands, were being evicted from their lodgings by the authorities, with no alternative accommodation, their possessions dumped onto pavements. The Reverend Sigamany, a prominent figure in the Indian community, arranged for these desperate people to take up accommodation at a military barracks in Lenz.

First Moves

Many of the newcomers to Lenasia were waiters at hotels and restaurants in the city centre who could not afford even moderate rentals, and found the lodgings at the military camp based 35km southwest of Johannesburg, affordable. It was a practical answer to an urgent need. They moved there in the early 1950s, living in barracks that were partitioned off into makeshift units.

The surrounding property was owned by a German national by the name of Lenz. He had acquired the property and settled there much earlier but he eventually sold the property to the government for housing developments.

At first, the entirety of Lenasia consisted of the people living at the barracks. Later the government sold plots for around R60 each, in the first extension to be established. The plots were purchased by families eligible for government loans to build private homes, according to strict specifications.

By 1955, the first school was established, the Lenasia High School, which was also meant to cater to Indian pupils living in Fordsburg and other areas of Johannesburg. These students would travel by train or bus to the school, the government having closed off access to high schools in Johannesburg. The first school principal, Mr Francis, was an enlightened educator, who served in this capacity from 1955 to 1967.

Like the other schools that followed, Lenz High School was a structure made up of asbestos, in an age when the dangers of the material had not been publicised. Despite the apparent temporary nature of the structure, it was used for some 40 years before a more permanent brick construction was erected, on another site, after the coming of democracy.

Indeed, infrastructure in Lenasia, in 1955, was nonexistent. Until the later 1950s, houses in Extension 1 had no piped water, electricity or sewage, except for a bucket system. Later a single U-shaped street became the first residential area proper. It was called 12th Street, and today it makes up Nightingale, into Sunbird, into Smew. The first families with permanent houses all lived along this horseshoe arrangement. Breadwinners travelled to the city centre via a road that crossed the railway line and connected with the R29 road that linked Johannesburg to Potchefstroom – mainly by a municipal bus service that offered two trips in the morning and two in the evening.

In 1958 Lenasia was proclaimed an Indian township under the Group Areas Act. The minutes of a meeting of the Non-European Affairs Committee of the Johannesburg City Council, dated 31 October 1961, reflect that the item under consideration was "Indian Housing: Lenz Camp". The minutes record that on 27 June 1961, the Council resolved that:

"(a) That the lease of part of the military camp at Lenz by the Council from the Group Areas Development Board be renewed for a period of six months as from 1st july 1961, on the same terms and conditions. (b) That the arrangement be subject to review after December 1961."

The minutes further record that the Secretary for Community Development had informed the Town Clerk in September that the Group Area Development Board was planning to take over the camp "as from 1st January 1962 on expiry of the present lease". The meeting ended with the recommendation:

"That the Group Area Development Board be asked to continue housing the existing tenants at the Lenz Camp until other accommodation becomes available for them."

Some of the earliest inhabitants include the Singh family from Sophiatown, the Adjoodas, Govenders, Moonsammys, and Khans, among others.

In 1957 Mr Bila Singh and his family moved to Lenasia Ext One after they were granted several plots on which to build homes. The Singhs were one of the pioneers on this new frontier, and continue to have a large presence in the town.

Mr Bila Singh, the oldest of a family with 10 siblings, reports that he was paid a sum for his property in Sophiatown that enabled him to qualify for a mortgage to build a house in Extension 1. Mr Singh said that the conditions in Sophiatown, which his family had abided because of an absence of alternatives, were horrendous. In his case, his father and his father's brother each had 10 children, and the entire household of some 24 people lived in two rooms. There was no privacy, the surrounding community had the use of only two toilets, the backyards were always filled with strangers, and life was near intolerable.

The creation of Lenasia meant that Indians were hived off into a separate area, and if Africans had a presence in the town, it was as workers: domestics or labourers. It also meant that Indians, as Mr Bila Singh reports, could "maintain their identity", ordering the environment in accordance with their religious and cultural practices.

But this development also meant that a process of differentiation took root, where Hindus and Muslims each developed a sometimes uneasy cohesion. Further divisions also became marked, to a large extent determined by class and caste stratification: Gujerati Hindus tended to have a more middle class position than Hindus of Tamil origin, while Muslims were stratified according to their place of origin in India, the well-known "gaam" system. Tamilian Hindus largely originated from indentured labourers, while Gujerati Hindus had earlier made their own passage to South Africa, as did many Muslims also from Gujerat.

The centre takes shape: Extension 2

When the number of those who could not qualify for houses on the mortgage scheme reached a certain critical mass, the government built council houses and other forms of residential units to house them. Thus, Greyville, Thomsville and Rainbow came into being, together making up Extension Two.

The units in Thomsville were basic, smaller even than the "matchbox" houses in Greyville. About six families were housed in one long structure, divided into six units of two rooms each. Toilets were shared, situated in the backyard. These were subeconomic units that housed the very poor, and it was no coincidence that many Thomsville residents were the offspring of indentured labourers.

Housing units in the Greyville section were a little more conducive to family life. Identical to the famous matchbox houses provided for African people in Soweto, they consisted of a kitchen, bathroom/toilet and three tiny bedrooms. Larger council houses were also provided for families that could be described as relatively middle-class, in what became known as Rainbow, also a part of Ext Two. Because the houses were painted in a variety of colours, residents spontaneously named the area Rainbow. These units consisted of 500 sq/m plots with three-bedroomed houses. They were occupied in 1962, when many people moved to Lenasia from Fordsburg and other areas.

The establishment of Extension 2 cemented the idea of an Indian township, and henceforth the idea of Lenasia took on a momentum that could not be reversed.

Further Extensions

The late 1970 and 1980s saw a massive migration to Lenasia. Housing estates were developed on a large scale and various extensions were added to the existing layout. Extension 3 opened up the east side of 1st Street, later renamed Flamingo Street. The houses were slightly more modern in appearance than the units in Rainbow. Ext 5 consisted of houses built on larger plots of 750 sq metres. Residents named the new swankier area "Luxury".

By late 1970, another extension was in the pipeline. The Johannesburg City Council noted at a meeting on 27 October 1970, that the Director of Local Government had made an application for permission to establish another residential area, Extension 6. It would be situated south of Extensions 2 and 4, and Department of Community Development plans set aside sites for two schools, two nursery schools, a business site, 27 sites for industrial purposes, and sites for a church, two parks and a cemetery. Water reticulation and electrical supplies were to be put in place.

Eventually, Lenasia grew to have 11 extensions, but the largest development came in 1984, when Lenasia South was established.

Leisure and infrastructure development

The houses in Ext One were built before water was piped into the area, and residents recall that a bucket system was in place to remove sewage. Electricity became available in the late 1950s, and the minutes of a Johannesburg City Council meeting on 27 January 1970 reveal that the council recommended "that Escom continues to give bulk supply to Lenasia for an indefinite period after incorporation" into the municipality.

In contrast, the houses in Rainbow were built only after an infrastructural grid was put in place, and residents moved into units equipped with water and electricity.

A Post Office was erected in the early 1960s, and a telephone exchange followed soon after. The early telephones were of the ring-the-exchange variety: the handsets did not have the round, numbered wheel that came later, and users had to rotate a lever that workers at the telephone exchange would answer – if they were awake – and put users through after they dialled the numbers to make the connection.

The Post Office also provided more affluent Lenasians with post boxes, from which they could collect their mail.

Sporting facilities were situated at a central point , next to the Lenasia High School. The grounds were used for soccer and cricket matches. In December 1969 the Lenasia Consultative Committee "expressed a wish to rename the Lenasia Sports Stadium after Mr W Lever as a gesture of esteem and gratitude for outstanding services rendered by him to the Indian Community of Lenasia during his term of office as representative of the Transvaal Board for the Development of Peri-Urban Areas". A meeting of the CC on 30 June 1970 resolved that the stadium be renamed the Wilfred Lever Stadium, and a sign be erected to indicate the new name.

A little earlier, a meeting of the JCC in March 1970 records that "there are certain sportsfields in Lenasia that require urgent maintenance. An Inter-Provincial cricket tournament is to be played on them early in March." The council recommended that R2000 be set aside for the maintenance of the sportsfields.

At a special meeting of the JCC, attended by members of the Management Committee, the Coloured Management Committee and the Lenasia Indian Consultative Committee, the council recommended that money be set aside for infrastructure developments in Coloured areas, and that recreation facilities in Lenasia be increased and upgraded. The council planned to spend R142 000 on a stadium, tennis courts, change rooms, playgrounds and equipment. A meeting in November records that a cricket oval, five open sportsfields, four tennis courts and two children's playgrounds would be constructed.

The council set aside R39000 for installing stormwater drainage in various areas in Ext 1, saying that "this stormwater drain is required as a matter of urgency to prevent the flooding of property".

On 23 February 1971, a special meeting of the City Council was convened to consider an application for borrowing powers for the construction of a Civic Centre. The council noted that there was a "pressing need in Lenasia for the public hall, library and administrative offices". It had received two tenders from Everest Construction Ltd and L Cohen Construction Ltd for the construction of the facilities. The Everest tender was accepted, at a cost of R254 500, and additional borrowing powers were granted.

By mid-1972, the Civic Centre was nearing completion, and on 29 August 1972, the JCC set charges for the hire of the hall. The council set the amounts at R25 for a five-hour period during weekdays, and R30 for weekends, including a deposit of R30. The smaller hall was to be hired out for R10 per session, including a deposit of R10.

Meanwhile, the growth of the township meant that the street names and house-number system was creating confusion. The Lenasia Indian Commercial Association wrote a letter to the Transvaal Peri-Urban Board on 23 April 1969, saying:

"Could you NOT take a second look at the system you have employed in naming and numbering the streets and avenues in this large Indian Township of Lenasia.

It is NOT only the police, postal or government departments that have a hard time in tracking down defaulter or addressee; business people and visitors to the area have an equally rough time in getting to their destination. If we could be of any assistance, may we say that the Authorities eliminate compass directions from the addresses of Lenasia and avoid duplicity in street and avenue numbers.

Trusting that this constructive suggestion will be worthy of consideration."

Their respectful suggestion was accepted by the Peri-Urban Board, which drew up and presented a report, dated 27 August 1969, to the JCC which was adopted by the council on 25 May 1971.

The Board illustrated the issue by saying, among other things, that "Honeysuckle Avenue connects up in a straight line with Ninth Street".

The Board had considered the issue and decided to rename the streets, deciding on the names of trees and flowers for Extensions 2 and 3, and birds for the other streets. Thus First Avenue became Rose Avenue, Seventh Avenue West and The Boulevard North became

Hummingbird Avenue. In all, 50 streets were renamed, reflecting the growth of the township.

In November 1971 the Council approved applications from people wanting to build additional rooms on their council properties, reflecting the growth of families and increased subletting. A 1970 census revealed that 43,8% of houses accommodated more than one family.

A September 1972 meeting of the Council considered the construction of a pleasure resort – noting that "this project is urgently needed by the Lenasia community because of a complete lack of this amenity in this area – and a swimming pool.

In November 1972 the Director of Local Government passed on a request to Council to set aside land between Lenasia and Lawley for a drive-in cinema. The Council approved the measure and the drive-in cinema was duly established, giving Lenasians one more facility to keep them in their Group Area. The Council minutes note that "the applicant wishes to establish a drive-in cinema to be used by the Indian population only", ruling out patrons from Soweto and Kliptown.

On 29 May 1973, the Council approved a recommendation from the management Committee to set aside an additional R9720 to complete stormwater drains on Rose Avenue.

After the Soweto students protest on 16 June 1976, the City Council allocated R4,25-million for the development of recreational facilities, the construction of a hospital, a medical day-care centre and a police station, all to be completed by 1980.

Top Shops: Commercial Activity
The beginnings of commercial activity were small. The Govender family operated a sort of tuck-shop at the railway station, as well as a coal business.

By the early 1960s a thriving commercial hub, known as Top Shops by residents, was developing, and shops were doing a more or less brisk trade in the business district, situated between Ext One, Greyville, Rainbow and Township.

Described in a 2004 Department of Finance and Economic Development report as poorly planned business district, a concentric arrangement of one-way streets makes for a discontinuous relation to the residential areas.

By the late 1960s Lenasia had its first cinema, Apsara Cinema. By 1970 another cinema known as Tahiti Cinema was constructed, next to the Tahiti shopping centre which was owned by a Mr O Joosub. JCC records reveal that the Council resolved in March 1970 to lease office space from Mr Joosub to set up administration offices after Lenasia's incorporation into the municipality.

The business district has extended southward, but cannot grow because westward expansion has never been possible because of the railway and the 675 000 square metre Lenz Military Base on the other side of the rail line. The LBD is boxed-in in the north and East by residential areas.

Over the years Lenasia has benefited from its proximity with Soweto. According to the 2004 Department of Finance and Economic Development report: "Residents of Lenasia proper generate about 42% of turnover, according to business owners. About 24% of patrons originate in Soweto. The remaining 35% of patrons originate in a broad geographic area ranging from north of Soweto to south of Orange Farm, and into Sedibeng and neighbouring jurisdictions."

The development of transport hubs has been welcomed and reviled. While shoppers from Soweto began to have easier access to shopping facilities in Lenasia, many saw the taxis as adding to already critical congestion.

Schools for toddlers
After the establishment of Lenasia High School, more schools were established to cater to the needs of a growing population. First

Primary became operational in the early 1960s, and Model Primary followed soon after. Nirvana High School was followed by Trinity High and the MH Joosub Technical School, as well as various primary schools.

A development of another kind indicates the growth of the township and its need for forms of regulation. Lenasia was assigned its own traffic police after Council created five posts for traffic inspectors. Council minutes report that "there have been repeated requests from the Indian Community of Lenasia for traffic control in this area. Motorists are disregarding traffic regulations and are not assisting in general safety. Dangerous conditions exist for school children who are obliged to cross busy roads on their way to and from school." The Council also opined that "Asian staff would be most suitable for this area".

The Council approved the purchase of six motor cycles for a sum of R7200 and set aside R4800 for the salaries of the five cops, who were to begin their duties on 1 February 1973.

Religious Developments
Religious developments exhibit the nature of the plurality that made up the Lenasia community. The subsections of the community began

to form religious organisations that mobilised their resources, most evident in the construction of churches, temples and mosques.

The first church, The Church of the Nazarine, was built in 1960 on the corner of 9th Street West and 10th Street West. Other churches followed, including the Anglican Church of Christ the Saviour (corner of Rose Ave and Petrea Str), the Church of St Thomas (Hummingbird Avenue), the Faith Evangelical Church Mission church (corner Rose Avenue and Dahlia Ave). The Christian community is relatively smaller than the other faith communities, but has always had a strong presence in the township.

The Hindu community has also set up a series of temples, one of the first being the Siva Soobramanian Temple on the corner of Primary and Heron Streets. Others include the Lakshmi Narayan Temple (Crane Street), the Sanathan Ved Dharma Sabha (Penguin Avenue).

The Rainbow Valley Mosque, situated in Lark Street (formerly 3rd Str South), was constructed on a residential site set aside for it in the midst of the council houses in Extension 2. Run by the Lenasia Muslim Association (LMA), it also included a madressah on the other half of the property.

The Saaberie Jumma Mosque was constructed in the early 1960s on the outskirts of Rainbow, on its border with Greyville in Rose Avenue.

Many other mosques emerged, including the Saaberie Chistie mosque, Nur-u Islam mosque, Jaamia mosque, Kuwait-ul Islam, Omar Farouk mosque, among others.

The Sporting Life
Right from the beginning, sport played a major role in forging a community spirit in Lenasia. Although other teams were already playing in various leagues, several teams became the most well-known and widely supported bodies in the bourgeoning town.

The Singh family, who had established the soccer team Swaraj even before they moved en-masse to Lenasia, became a central feature of life in Lenasia.

Later the Munsamy family, children of First Primary principal Mr Alan Munsammy, established Bluebells, perhaps the most popular of Lenasia's soccer teams. A fierce rivalry developed between the two main teams.

Dynamos, established in Ferreirastown in Johannesburg, also had a presence in Lenasia. Made up mostly of Muslim players, Dynamos was mostly supported by Muslims, while Swaraj drew mostly Hindu supporters and Bluebells mainly Tamil fans, although Bluebells somehow had a more cosmopolitan quality that saw people across the community give them their support.

These teams were embroiled in a system that encouraged ethnic and religious divisions within the community, but there were also attempts by some to diminish the influence of ethnicity and other divisive factors.

The Minister of Sport, Piet Koornhof, had been trying to construct a notion of "multiracial sport", as opposed to non-racial sport. Koornhof's plan was to keep sport divided along racial lines, but he presented the division as differences between nationalities – in line with separate development ideology.

When the Lenasia Football Association found itself under pressure to restrict footballing activities to Indians, it chose instead to pursue a non-racial approach. At an award presentation on 29 November 1974, Lenasia Management Committee chairman RAM Salojee congratulated the association on its stance.

Cricket also enjoyed much support in Lenasia, and various leagues were in existence. At first many local cricketers played for the Vredons, formed by Revrend Sigamony around 1935. They used the Natalspruit grounds. Later, Lenasians formed their own teams, including Surrey, Arsenals, Queensland and other cricket clubs. There was enough activity to support three divisions.

When the stadium was renamed the Varachia Stadium in the late 1970s, and Minister of Sport Piet Koornhof presided over the ceremony, activists and cricketers mounted protests. Varachia, the president of newly formed SA Cricket Union, was opposed by Sacos, the anti-apartheid sporting body.

Lenasia in the Democratic Era
With the coming of democracy, changes in the social fabric of Lenasia matched the changes in the social, political and economic structure of the country in general. The demise of apartheid meant that, theoretically at least, Lenasia was no longer an Indian Group Area. But the inertia of apartheid structures meant that it has effectively continued to be an Indian residential area, although some changes have become plain for all to see.

Migratory patterns have contributed to the transformation. Many residents, especially younger ones, have moved out of their home town to live closer to their workplaces in Johannesburg. Former Lenasians now live in Greenside, Emmarentia, Houghton, Midrand and many other areas formerly populated only by whites.

The influx of non-South African Asians from India, Bangladesh and especially Pakistan has hanged the nature of the township, introducing yet another element in a multicultural town.

Other developments have to do with the governing structures. No longer a Group Area, Lenasia now falls under region 11 of the Johannesburg Municipality, and falls under a new form of governance.

The passing of apartheid opened the way for scholars from Soweto and other African areas to attend schools in Lenasia. The development of a large informal settlement, Thembelihle, was also possible because of the new political dispensation.

Other changes have been indirect outcomes of the political transition. Lenasia, like Soweto, has come to be counted as a regional economy, and developers have stepped in to tap this market. Thus Lenasia now has its own mall, the Trade Route Mall, a huge shopping centre that features national franchises that make it unnecessary for residents to travel to the city centre to do their shopping.

Thembelihle Informal settlement

The demise of apartheid meant that influx control and segregation policies were no longer in place to dictate where people live. Since a large percentage of the population of Lenasia has always included domestic workers, there has always been an African presence in the town. Many of these workers prefer to have their own homes rather than live on the premises of their employers, and have set up shacks or small buildings in an area between Extensions 9 and 10, now known as Thembelihle.

The growth of the settlement has posed new challenges for the people of Lenasia and for governance structures. The people of Thembelihle have been clamouring for government to provide services to them, and have embarked on violent service delivery protests.

The Asian Influx
Lenasia has beome a favourite destination for migrants from India, Bangladesh and Pakistan. The majority of migrants are men aged between 18 and 40, with very few females among them. Most of these men are from rural areas in their home countries and have education levels up to high school, but rarely university degrees.

Many of them are employed in the informal sector and earn low wages, although some have started their own businesses, such as food stalls or takeaway shops, hairdressing salons, trading in small goods.

They tend to form networks that take care of needs such as accommodation. Many of them live in flats in Lenasia's business district, usually in large groups and in higher densities than locals would, splitting the rent into manageable portions.

The relationship between the older residents and the migrants is complex. It would be safe to say that the migrants do not pose competition for jobs, since they tend to inhabit a different class position and gravitate towards the informal sphere. They have begun to provide services that South Africans have begun to shy away from. The typical hairdresser in Lenasia is a dying breed, and Indians and Pakistanis have flocked to this profession, providing relatively cheap haircuts for men in many areas besides Lenasia.

The variety of cuisine has also grown, with migrants opening restaurants and take-away facilities featuring Tandoori menus which had not previously been available. Indeed, the many Indian restaurants in Johannesburg are staffed by many of these new migrants.

Official figures for Asian migrants, culled from the 2001 census, are widely thought to be lower than the actual number of migrants. A report by the Consortium of Refugees and Migrants in South Africa (CORMSA: 2008) estimated that there are 60 000 – 70 000 Pakistanis in the country and 30 000 – 40 000 Bangladeshis.

New South African Schooling
With the introduction of universal schooling in the new South Africa, the nature of the education system has changed. Previously falling under the House of Delegates, Lenasia's schools now fall under the Department of Education. Another change came with the introduction

of Outcomes Based Education (OBE) in 1997, which has proved to be a disastrous policy in practice, and has very recently been revoked.

With the deracialisation of education, scholars from Soweto flocked to Lenasia's schools, which they perceived as providing better teaching and other facilities. This was followed, or perhaps happened at the same time, as Indian scholars migrating to private schools in Lenasia and in formerly white areas.

The majority of pupils at schools in Lenasia are now African children from Lenasia's informal settlement, Themelihle, and from Soweto and surrounding areas. The children from Soweto can be seen boarding taxis when they return home, boosting the taxi industry in the area.

There has also been a change in the racial composition of teachers, with African teachers appointed to teach at Lenasia's schools. This follows the exodus of senior Indian teachers who were given retrenchment packages by the new government.

Younger Indian teachers have also found it difficult to cope with the transformations, especially with the introduction of OBE, which discourages rote learning and traditional forms of assessments. One effect of OBE has been that teachers find it difficult to teach numeracy skills, which depends on a certain amount of rote learning.

Other problems have also emerged like the large amount of paperwork which has become a discouraging factor and the fact that the pupils are not available for extra tuition because they live elsewhere further disheartens the teachers. Increased learner/teacher ratios has made it difficult to maintain classroom discipline and devote adequate levels of attention to each pupil, and language difficulties have also been reported. The lack of access to parents also makes it difficult to develop a relationship with the pupil.

The Ups and Downs of Business
A report commissioned by the Department of Finance and Economic Development explored the economic potential for Lenasia. It found that factors affecting the viability and functioning of the Lenasia business district (LBD) included "crime and grime, traffic and congestion poor access and visibility, lack of management resources, and an increasingly competitive retail environment".

The report concluded that the business district appeals to consumers on two basic levels: it has a strong focus on specialty goods related to Indian cultural patterns; and it features a high volume of discount shopping, attracting those with limited incomes.

Addressing the issue of the new Trade Routes Mall, it warned that competition would stiffen and the presence of national retailers, such as those that take up the majority of shops in the mall, would see traders in the business district losing significant market share.

But the report concludes that the business district, despite its poor location and various constraints, "is a viable economic entity" that can adjust to the new competition by building on its strengths: specialty and discount trading, as a cultural and entertainment hub, and through redevelopment.

Businesses in Lenasia are reliant on submarket – shoppers from Soweto and Eldorado Park, as well as areas such as Ennerdale, south of Lenasia. The presence of the army in the Lenz Military camp means that soldiers also do their shopping in Lenasia.

About 80% of businesses in the LBD engage in retail trade, about 9% on auto maintenance and repair, 5,5% for medical services, 3,5% for financial and banking services, and 2% for professional services such as engineers, lawyers and architects. About 3120 people work in the LBD.

Approximately 250 residential units, mostly flats, are located in the LBD, housing about 775 people. Businesses are also located in other sites in Lenasia, and Rose Avenue, probably the longest street in the town, has seen many residential units turned to business use, which has resulted in an increase in traffic congestion along the road. Open air public spaces are also used for business activities. The space across the road from the railway station has been used as a market, with as many as 600 stalls doing trade, a significant number of them informal traders.

Lenasia is now home to two large shopping centres, Signet Terrace and the Trade Routes Mall. Other shopping centres include the Freeway Plaza Area close to the eastern highway exit, the Protea/Nirvana node, Nirvana Circle at the intersection of Nirvana Drive and Flamingo Road, and the LTA Plaza in Extension 2 at the intersection of Impala Street and Rose Avenue.

Three main industrial areas are located near the business district:

Albert Street Industrial Area
Situated in Extension 6, the area had 27 enterprises engaged in construction, food processing, auto repair, warehousing, metalwork and printing.

Anchorville Industrial park

Located about 2km south of Lenasia, 28 firms were based in Anchorville in 2002, engaged in cosmetics, construction, furniture, food processing, plasticware, metalworks, warehousing and auto repair and maintenance. About 500 people work in Anchorville.

Lawley Industrial Area

Although underdeveloped, the majority of the area is used by Corobrick, which manufactures bricks for regional and national distribution. Corobrick employs 250 people and produces 200 000 bricks a day, seven days a week. It began operating in 1988 and is expected to continue operating until around 2030 or even later.

A dumpsite is also located in Lawley, owned by Pikitup.

New Malls, New Lifestyles
The emergence of Signet Terrace Shopping Centre, in Gemsbok Street, on the site of the original Lenasia High School, has transformed the business district as well as the culture of the township. As a site for many national franchises, Lenasians now often eat out at the many restaurants, a practice that had not existed before because of the dearth of restaurants and the predominance of take-away joints.

This trend was reinforced by the inauguration of the Trade Route Mall in 2009. Now Lenasia has a spread of business areas, and the local economy has been transformed by the new developments. There are more people employed within Lenasia than ever before, and less of Lenasians' money leaves the township.

A 2001 census found that residents of Lenasia work throughout Johannesburg, especially in the Johannesburg CBD. The breakdown:

SECTOR	PERCENTAGE OF WORKFORCE IN SECTOR
Retail	30%
Finance	22%
Social services	21%
Manufacturing	17%
Mining	1%

Year	Population
1960	650
1970	21037
1996	48211
2001	54457
2010	+/- 60 000

The development of malls in Soweto, though, means that shoppers from the township are less likely to shop in Lenasia than they used to be, and although figures are hard to come by, the trend has been noticed by some business people. The population of Lenasia has grown to such an extent that it is a significant nodal point in the Johannesburg metropolis. Figures reveal a huge influx in the later 1960s and 1970s, when the Group Areas policy was at its height:

Politics and Governance

As alluded to throughout this brief history, the move to Lenasia was from the very beginnings determined by political events and policies. The first to settle were grateful that they had been provided with accommodation that far surpassed their previous conditions in terms of living space, access to basic conditions and possibility for development. As such, many came under the sway of government influence, and worked hand in hand with apartheid authorities, wittingly or unwittingly.

But many were opposed to the grand designs of apartheid, even if they had been forced to succumb to decisions made under the Group Areas Act and other apartheid legislation.

Apartheid Politics

The South African Indian Council was established by the state in 1964. An advisory body without any decision-making powers, its members were appointed by the state, and their lack of representivity weakened their capacity from the beginning.

The Lenasia Indian Consultative Committee was established in 1964. The minutes of a Management Committee meeting held on 5 November 1969 reveal that on 15 April 1964, "a consultative committee system of local government was established by the Hon. The Administrator ... for the Indian Group Area of Lenasia".

The Committee carried out its functions "under the jurisdiction of the Transvaal Board for the Development of Peri-Urban Areas". It consisted of five members appointed by the Administrator who met once a month. But after Lenasia would be incorporated into the Johannesburg Municipality on 1 January 1970, "the functions and responsibilities of this committee will have to be carried out under the jurisdiction of the Council".

The minutes also report that "secretarial and other administrative duties in Lenasia are being undertaken by Mr D Rathinasamy, an official of the Transvaal Board for the Development of Peri-Urban Areas". The five members of the committee were V Govender (chairman), O Joosub (vice-chairman), C Pillay, SM Vania and S Govender. V Govender and IFH Mayet were also sitting members of the SA Indian Council.

The members of the committee were not paid, and enjoyed no executive powers. They operated until a few years after Lenasia's incorporation into the Johannesburg Municipality in 1970.

The terms of office of the Consultative Committee expired on 21 October 1970, and the committee was reconstituted in November

1970. The new committee would have five members, two appointed by the Minister of Community Development and one by Council. The Council recommended that S Govender be appointed, with O Joosub as an alternate.

In April 1972, the Council agreed to pay the members of the committee allowances of R50 for the chairman and R40 for other members, backdated to 1 November 1971.

Plans had been underway for the government to reconstitute the Lenasia Indian Consultative Committee as a Management Committee, and on 30 May 1972, the City Council considered the issue in more detail, with input from an Ad Hoc Committee for Indian Affairs. The new system would see representatives elected, with the vote being given to residents aged 21 and older.

When the Coloured Management Committee decided on 16 April 1972 to ask the Council to provide its members with tokens of office so that they could be identified as committee members, the Council decided to manufacture medallions for this purpose. The members of Lenasia's Management Committee would also receive this privilege. The Council resolved to get two companies to manufacture chairman's medallions and members' lapels, to be plated in 9 carat gold.

Council moved on its plans for a management Committee after receiving a letter from the Director of Local Government requesting that the Council submit "proposals for a partly elected and partly nominated Committee". The Council on 27 February 1973 resolved:

"Voting qualifications were made as simple as possible to allow all adults of the age of eighteen years and over to register as voters, and 7609 applications were received by the closing date of 31 December 1972. This represents about fort percent of the number of voters estimated to be eligible."

The Council determined that six candidates would be elected and three nominated.

The Council had also set into motion the process of determining wards, and on 27 March 1973 it recommended approval of six wards, and on 29 May set the date for the election as Wednesday, 12 September 1973.

Dr RAM Salojee, who had been one of the founders of the Lenasia Residents and Ratepayers Association, formed the Peoples Candidate Party to contest elections for the local council. He sought the endorsement of Lenasians at a public meeting in 1973, attended by hundreds of supporters. The subsequent poll, with a 75% turnout, returned Dr Salojee to the top position in the management committee.

Salojee, by many accounts a well-intentioned general practitioner and community leader, had decided to take part in the government organised structure because he wanted to minister to the needs of the community, and because he wanted to prevent positions of influence falling into the hands of corrupt, self-serving opportunists. But Salojee was criticised by more radical anti-apartheid elements, such as the Black Consciousness activists and some Congress-aligned figures.

Salojee served on the Management Committee for a little more than one term, but arrived at the conclusion that working within the system yielded no benefits for the community, and from then on boycotted government-created institutions. Later, in the 1980s, he became the Vice-President of the Anti-SAIC Committee, as well as a vice president of the UDF's Transvaal Region, throwing in his lot with Congress-aligned organisations.

Organisations allied to the ANC, such as the Transvaal Indian Congress, were banned in the wake of Sharpeville and the Treason and Rivonia trials. But Congress-affiliated activities did take place, despite the ban on the ANC. When Ahmed Timol, an ANC operative, was killed while in detention in 1971, Lenasia's residents held a meeting in his honour, and hundreds attended.

But by the late 1960s, Black Consciousness became the dominant anti-apartheid ideology in many African, Indian and Coloured schools and universities, and had a number of adherents in Lenasia. The charismatic Sadeque Variava, a student at the Teachers Training College in Fordsburg and a resident of Lenasia, spearheaded the dissemination of BC ideology in the town. He mobilised several people into a potent BC grouping, including Rashid Moosa (the older brother of Mohammed Valli Moosa), Ebrahim "Tibu" Mayet, and various other young comrades.

The group formed the Lenasia Students Movement and the People's Experimental Theatre (PET), which staged various theatre productions in the township.

The Barn Incident

October 1977 was a momentous month in the politics of South Africa. Following the unrest of June 1976, and continuous unrest in many townships and schools across the country, the State decided to crack down on all Black Consciousness organisations. The move came after security police effectively killed BC leader Steve Biko on 12 October, this sparked a wave of revulsion across the country as well as the international community. On 19 October the State declared 18 BC organisations unlawful and banned two newspapers, the World and the Weekend World.

In Lenasia, where political activity had been disrupted by the arrest of the BC leaders, several young people felt the need to express their outrage at the death of Biko and the bannings, and organised a protest meeting set for Saturday 21 October. Led by Anjeni Poonan, Rooha Variava and Haroon Patel, the students distributed pamphlets at schools calling for students to register their outrage.

When the students gathered at the venue, the owner of the hall could not be found, and Patel began to address the students. Some weeks earlier, the State had declared all open-air gatherings illegal, and some later felt that they had been set up, forced to hold the meeting in the open air, thus rendering them liable for arrest.

Patel had barely begun to speak when scores of police stormed the venue, beating the students and assaulting many, including young girls. The police had effectively sealed off the venue, and no one could escape. They were taken to Protea Magistrates Court in Soweto and processed before being moved to John Vorster Square in the Joburg city centre. They were locked up in cells, girls in the one and boys in the other.

After three nights in prison, they were charged and released after pleading guilty.

Those who attended the meeting include Hassan Lorgat, Agsie Pillay, Gregs Moonsamy and many others, in total between 40 and 50 people. Some suffered severe consequences. Linda Moonsamy, Haroon Bera, Hassen Lorgat and nine others, who had been enrolled at the Transvaal Indian College of Education in Fordsburg, were expelled. Teacher Yusuf "Luke" Kajee, who was one of the only adults at the meeting, suffered from persistent harassment by the education department.

Many of those who attended the meeting later continued, in various forms and through myriad organisation, the struggle against apartheid.

Time to Learn

Students influenced by Black Consciousness, led by Hassan Lorgat and Haroon Bera, set up an extra-curricular tuition scheme, where students were helped with homework and with extra lessons by volunteers, mostly university students and teachers. But the students received more than school lessons, they were also politicised in the process, in an application of the "conscientising" method propagated by BC strategists.

Operating at the Jiswa Centre, school children of all ages could attend classes every afternoon, and hundreds of them passed through the facility. Many of them eventually peopled the local and national anti-apartheid organisations that emerged later.

The 1980 Schools Boycotts

The school boycotts of 1980 began in February at Mountainview High School in Cape Town. Coloured school-goers, having become politicised by ongoing discrimination, rejected the educational designs of the apartheid planners. By April the boycott had spread to the Cape Flats, and to the Transvaal, where 2000 students went on a march. Solidarity marches began to take place in Natal, as well as other parts of the country.

In Lenasia it was the students of Nirvana High that first began to protest, on 22 April, to be joined the next day by students at Lenasia High, Trinity and MH Joosub Technical College.

The students were briefed by older activists such as Yusuf "Joe" Veriava, Jerry Waja (both of the BC movement) as well as Congress people such as Kanti Parshotam, Mohammed Valli Moosa, Ismail Momoniat, Ismail Vadi (a new generation of Congress activists) and Reggie Vandeyar, who served a decade on Robben Island.

Students leading the movement included Saffora Sadeck, Kenneth Sebastian and Shamim Akhalwaya from Nirvana, Haroon Krull and Mickie Padayachee from MH Joosub, and Mohsin Moosa, Rashid Seedat and Yasmin Momoniat at Lenasia High.

The students organised committees at each school and forged links with students at Coloured schools in Bosmont, Riverlea and Eldorado Park.

A Parents Action Committee was established to help and guide the students and to convince cautious parents to support their children. The Committee included Joe Veriava, Dr Essop Jassat, Cassim Saloojee, Joe Cassim and Dr Yusuf Saloogee. The committee published a newsletter, called 'Cause', which set out their grievances.

By June 1980 the boycotts had petered out. Several members of the community were detained, including Joe Veriava, Ismail Momoniat, Mohammed Valli Moosa. Two teachers, Mr Y Essack and Solly Ismail were also detained as well as students, including Rajesh Cheebur, Yusuf Jada, Zunaid Mohammed and Firdoze Bulbulia from Trinity High; Haroon Krull, Kenny Padayachie, Sharon Pillay, Ashwin Moyenie, Nazir Omar and Fuad Abrahams from MH Joosub Tech; Jitendra Hargovan; and Kenneth Sebastian from Nirvana High.

Congress Politics Resurgent

In 1979, tensions between BC and Congress forces came to a head when Congress activists managed to displace BC leaders from the Anti-SAIC bodies. Previously, both streams had been part of anti-SAIC efforts, but at a crucial meeting at Jiswa to elect an Anti-SAIC Committee, Congress activists were elected to run the organisation. Essop Jassat was voted chairman, RAM Salojee became Vice Chairman, and Ismail Momoniat was made the secretary.

With the decline of the BC organisations, which had been banned in October 1977, and the banning of many of its leaders, ANC-affiliated activists began to mobilise in Lenasia, avoiding the kinds of errors made by BC activists, and linking everyday struggles to political issues in order to mobilise entire communities rather than small sector of the intelligentsia, as the BC activists had been doing.

A civic movement emerged, and Congress activists organised residents committees, transport committees, and organisations focussing on the everyday struggles of ordinary Lenasians.

The year 1980 marked the 25th anniversary of the emergence of the Freedom Charter, which renewed focus on the philosophy, politics and symbols of the Congress movement.

The trade union movement was also re-emerging after the wave of industrial unrest in Durban in 1973. Activists called for people to boycott various products whose manufacturers were being challenged by trade unionists. Thus, campaigns to boycott red meat, Wilson Rowntree and Fattis and Monis products emerged.

When the government announced that elections would be held in 1981 for positions on the SAIC, the move was opposed on a mass scale, and the Transvaal Anti-SAIC Committee (TASC) took as its task the boycott of the elections.

When they held a rally in August 1981, 3000 people attended the meeting. Even the activists were shocked at the turnout. The wife of Walter Sisulu, Albertina Sisulu, was the main speaker at the event.

The election, held on 4 November, was boycotted by the majority of eligible voters. Polls in some areas were ridiculously low: in Fordsburg two votes were cast, and in Lenasia only 10% of voters cast votes. The security police swooped on congress activists, detaining Prema Naidoo, Shirish Nanabai and Ismail Momoniat from Lenasia, and Firoz Cachalia from Benoni.

The Congress activists decided that a more permanent structure was needed to continue mobilising anti-apartheid forces, especially since the Botha regime was in the process of establishing the Tricameral Parliament as part of its constitutional reforms, and revived the Transvaal Indian Congress (TIC). The move was heavily contested and became a source of tensions between Congress organisations and those aligned to BC and ultra-left organisations.

The TIC was formally reconstituted at a meeting held in the Ramkrishna Hall in Lenasia on 1 May 1983.

Indian education in Natal

1865

A report? Native Schools 1865? states that these were day and evening schools.Á, There was a Mr Earl?s school on the Isipingo plantation which was attended by both Natives and Indians.

1867

20 September, Lieutenant Governor Keate in Despatch Number 47 of 1867 wrote that on the Reunion Estate a hospital was converted into a schoolroom for Indian children on the estate.

1865

A report ?Native Schools 1865? states that these were day and evening schools. There was a Mr Earl?s school on the Isipingo plantation which was attended by both Natives and Indians.

1867

20 September, Lieutenant Governor Keate in Despatch Number 47 of

1867 wrote that on the Reunion Estate a hospital was converted into a schoolroom for Indian children on the estate.

1868

In the Brooks 1868 Parliamentary Papers Vol. 18 states that the Reverend Ralph Stott established a day school for Indians in Durban.

1868

31 March, In the 1868 Native Affairs Report ? Vol 16 ?No. 26 states that there was Mr Barker?s school at Umzinto which was also attended by Natives and Indians. The school was an evening school.

1871

In a report by the Superintendent of Education in the 1871 Natal Blue Book (NBB) it is recorded that there was a school at the Lower Umkomanzi for Indian children on the sugar estate

1872

August, The Coolie Commission drew the attention of the Government to the necessity of educating Indians. The Commission?s papers stated that there was also an evening school on the Umgeni Estates.

1874

The Education Commission of 1874 recommended that the Government should assist owners and managers of plantations to maintain schools on plantations and that the Durban Corporation should cooperate with the Government in the immediate erection of schools in Durban. The Commission also recommended that all Indian children within a reasonable distance should be compelled to attend, under the direction and with the approval of the Protector of Indian immigrants. The Education Commission also said that the attendance of non-European children at European schools was approved by Lieutenant Governor Keate.

1875

27 August, Lieutenant Governor Keate stipulated that all schools in Natal aided by the Government were to be open to all classes.

1876

There were only two schools for Indians and both were in Durban. The first was a day school with 34 pupils and the second an evening school with 20 scholars.

1878

Up to 1877 no systematic effort had been made for the education of Indian children. Only in 1878 that Law of 20/1878 was passed making provision for a board of education called the Indian Immigrant School Board. The establishment of the Board created a dual system of education for Indians as they were allowed to attend European schools.

1879

26 March 1879, The first meeting of the Indian Immigration School Board was held in the office of the Protector of Indian Immigrants in Durban. Present were the Protector of Indian Immigrants, the Rev Ralph Stott and Mr Heury Binns, a planter. Not all members of the Board were present ? the meeting lasted two hours. The minutes of the Indian Immigration School Board states that a resolution was taken that an Inspector (Education) should be obtained from the Government of Madras, India. The School Board also resolved that aid should be given to schools established or conducted by private persons for the special instruction of Indian children

February 1879, The board sent a circular to employers of Indian labour in which they were asked for their opinions on the establishment and maintenance of schools and what support they would give towards the erection of schools on their estates. Only six replies were received.

1880

About sixty Indian children attend European schools in Natal.

1881

Out of 123 above the age of 15 at Government Schools, 37 were Indian.Mr George Dunning, formerly the headmaster of the High School, Chitaldrug, Madras Presidency, India was selected and he arrived in South Africaon on 9 September 1881.

15 October, Minutes of the Indian Immigration School Board reported that a Commission communicated with Mr Dunning to make a tour of inspection on the coast to acquire full information in connection with the educational needs of Indian. Mr Dunning visited several estates and submitted a report but the Board instructed him to prepare another report as it found the first one unsatisfactory.

26 November, Mr Dunning reported for the second time but that planters were dissatisfied.

5 April, The Victoria Planters Association passed a resolution that Mr Dunning was devoting too much attention to the education of the children of Indian indentured workers and did not look after the educational needs of the children of the Free Indians.

1881

5 April, The Victoria Planters Association passed a resolution that Mr Dunning was devoting too much attention to the education of the children of Indian indentured workers and did not look after the educational needs of the children of the Free Indians.1 August, The Board felt that Dunning?s work/report was unsatisfactory and gave him three months dismissal notice. Mr Colepeper, the acting Protector of the Indian Immigration was appointed inspector of Indian schools.

1883

The Railway school was the only departmental school attended mainly by the children of the Natal Government Railway employees.

1883

The Railway school was the only departmental school attended mainly by the children of the Natal Government Railway employees. Evening school for adults were held at the Durban Board School, the Railway School in Durban, the Umgeni School and the Equefa School.There were two private schools, the Umgeni Private School and the Mount Moriah Private School.

October, The first School Board was opened. Law 20 of 1878 empowered the Indian Immigration School Board to establish its own school.

November, An estate school was opened at Prospect Hall.

1884

Another estate school was opened at Clare Estate ?both these schools were mission schools. Dr Booth's school in Durban had over 100 pupils. A Mr Vinden?s Private School operated in Pietermaritzburg. The school was closed in 1885. By this year the total amount in grants given to Indian education was £626.5s.0d compared to £68 paid out in 1874. By the following year the only evening school that was well attended was the Railway School nearly all the evening schools had been closed, since workers in country places were too tired after their days work to attend evening school. Those in town had been prevented by the 9 o?clock curfew bell from attending.

12 July, According to the minutes of the Indian Immigration School Board school board minutes a proposal to establish a Board school in Pietermaritzburg but because the Pietermaritzburg Corporation meeting refused to provide a site for such a school it was decided no further steps should be taken in the establishment of such a school.

1885

Evening school were held at the Durban Bboard School, the Umgeni Board School, the Tongaat Board School, the Railway School Board, Verulam, Isipingo, Avoca, Umzinto, Durban (Rev. H. Stott) and Pietermaritzburg (Rev.J.Barret). The Indian Immigration School Board considered the introduction of women from the Zenana Missions in

India for the purpose of educating Indian girls in Durban and Pietermaritzburg.

1888

Rocks, an Indian, operated the Private Adventure School in Pietermaritzburg. It was closed in 1889.

April, A girls? school was opened in Durban under the management of Dr Booth.

1889

The Tongaat Board School which had been established in the midst of a large population of free Indians was closed since a properly qualified teacher could not be found .It was then re-opened as an aided school under the management of Dr Booth. A new school for girls was opened in Pietermaritzburg under the Rev Swabey.

1890

Sea Cow Lake Private Adventure School opened. It closed in 1891.

1891

In a report on Native Education in the Natal Blue Book, it was reported that Indians also attended the St Frances Xavier Native School.

1892

Another school for girls, also under the management of Dr Booth was opened in Durban as well as the Umbilo Girls School in Durban.

1894

22 February, Mr Jameson seconded by a Mr Johnson moved in the Council of Education a motion, ?That is any neighbourhood where an Indian or Native school is established, children of these nationalities be not admitted to government schools as free pupils.?

1897

There were only two government schools for Indians, one in Durban and the other at Umgeni.

1899

February, The first higher grade school for Indians was established in Durban under Act No.7 of 1899. It was opened in a room in Alice Street. There were 38 boys on the register when the school opened. The government refused Indian boys admission to European schools.

1902

According to the Colonial Indians News (14/02/1902 - A New Hindu School), owing to the deep seated ill-feeling among the Hindus, e.g. against the proselytising propaganda of missionary teachers. Hindus resolved not to send their children to schools established under the control of missionaries. Thus they established a school in Pietermaritzburg.

October, The government opened a higher grade school in Pietermaritzburg only after repeated representations.

1904

It was stated that no grants was to be paid to Native children attending Indian school that were within reasonable distance of Native Aided Schools.

1905

Indian infants and girls were dismissed from European school. They were to be accommodated at the Higher Grade School. At the end of this year, infants and girls at the Durban Higher Grade School were dismissed. The Indian community protested.

August, Indian infants and girls were dismissed from European school. They were to be accommodated at the Higher Grade School.

4 September, The Carlisle Street School was opened for Indian and Coloured youth.

1906

2 February, The dismissed pupils were readmitted and taught separately, as before, from the senior boys by a woman teacher. The annual report of the Education Department stated that over 3 000 Indian children were being educated in five government schools and 27 aided schools.

1907

August, The infant class and standard one classes were abolished and the school started from standard two.

1908

24 July, Indians protested against the abolition of the infants? class and standard one but the Government would not entertain the petition.

1909

The title High Grade School was abolished and the name ? Indian School under the charge of European Teachers? adopted.

1 February, No pupil under five or over fourteen years of age was to be admitted to Government School for Indians.

April, According to Government Notice No. 201/1909 of 23 April 1909, Section 3 stated that no Native, Indian or Coloured children were to be admitted to schools ,other than those provided for them. Section 38 stipulated that no subject, not included in the standard syllabus of primary schools taught during ordinary school hours in Indian schools under the charge of European teachers. This was presumably meant to prevent the teaching of the vernacular or other subjects to foster Indian religion.

15 May, Indians protested against the age restriction and that at Indian schools children were had been denied the benefits of free education.

July, At a meeting held in Pietermaritzburg it was unanimously decided that a private high school should be opened here for those children who had been refused admission to Government Higher Grade Schools by the age limit of 14 years and by the neglect of the Government to provide facilities for higher education for Indians.

1 August, A private high school (in Pietermaritzburg) to meet the requirements of the Indian community in connection with higher education was opened. The school was under the control of a Committee of five members who received financial support from the Indian public. The fees were fixed at five shillings per boy and 10 shillings for the children of Indians from the same family.

October, There were 13 children at this school; six boys were being trained for the Cape Junior University Examination and the remainder for the Cape Elementary Examination.

17 December, An Arab trader whose son had been excluded from attendance at the school brought an action before the Supreme Court to test the legality of the age restriction. Judgement was on this date, but the action failed.

1910

There were only five government schools in Natal ? four in Durban and one in Pietermaritzburg.The Durban Anjuman Islam School was opened as another Indian initiative in education as a result of the Government?s restriction on Government?s schools for Indians.

1911

1 September, The Indian Educational Institute was opened in Durban by private initiative. At first it was intended for day scholars only, but after some delay an evening class was provided. The evening class made provision for tuition in Indian languages and commercial subjects. The number of scholars increased from 23 in Jan 1912 to 30 in March 1916.The fees were £1.1s per pupil per month.

1915

382 children in Indian schools received free tuition and books or either the one or the other.

1916

The Indian Educational Institute eventually closed down.

1917

By this year the Education Department was educating only 1/5 of the Indian school song population.

1918

1 August, The Indian community asked the Education Department whether provisions could not be made by forming a special class for higher education at the school formerly called the Durban Higher Grade School if a separate institution could not be provided for higher education. Such a class was started at the Carlisle Street Government School.

1922

20 April, A report of the Education Committee of this date considered it not the duty of the State to give instruction through the medium of a language that was foreign to the country.

1926

A Select Committee announced its inability to make any recommendations in connection with vernacular education. The policy of Anglicisation remained.

1927

Nine Europe women teachers were employed at the Carlisle Street

School in Durban. There were no facilities for industrial training except at the York Road School in Pietermaritzburg which provided tuition in woodwork.

November, Two education experts, Mr Kailas P. Kichlu (M.A), Deputy Director of Public Instruction from the United Province of Agra and Oudh and Vice Chancellor of the University of Agra and Miss C. Gordon, (Bachelor of Education) Professional Teachers Training College, Saidapet, Madras arrived in the Union and took up residence in Natal where they studied the ?Problems? of Indian education with the help of the Education Department, Indian teachers and the leaders of the local Indian community. They also toured much of Natal.

1928

The Kichlu Memorandum (paragraphs 26 and 28) stated that the Indian community had already spent large sums of money on school buildings. In comparison with the £50 000-00 spent by Indians on Aided and Private schools, the Government had spent, from 1910 to 1928, on Government and Aided schools, only £22,843.00.

By this year, of the nine Government schools, only the Carlisle Street School, which had then just been raised to the Matriculation standard, taught up to standard X, the remaining eight Government schools were primary schools.

January 1928, The South African Indian Congress (S.A.I.C) passed a resolution requesting that the Union Government provide facilities for Technical, Industrial and Agriculture education. The resolution was then forwarded to the Administrators of the Transvaal, Natal and the Cape Province. That portion which referred to Technological Education was submitted to the Technical Colleges. The Natal Technical College in Durban could not find accommodation and did not have the necessary funds for capital and current expenditure. The Technical College in Pietermaritzburg submitted a similar reply.

December, The first trade union congress organised by the officials of the Natal Indian Congress (NIC) asked the Union Government to provide technical education for Indian apprentices or that Indian apprentices should be exempted from technical education as required by the Apprenticeship Act.

1929

The Kichlu Memorandum (paragraphs 26 and 28) stated that the Indian community had already spent large sums of money on school buildings. In comparison with the £50 000-00 spent by Indians on Aided and Private schools, the Government had spent, from 1910 to1928, on Government and Aided schools, only £22,843.00.

1930

Provision was made for bursaries for Indian students tenable at the Fort Hare Native College. There were 69 (community) Aided schools against the 13 Government schools. **1 February,** Sastri College was opened in Durban. It was named after V.S. Srinivasa Sastri, the Indian Agent, who had proposed an educational institute in Durban to be erected and equipped solely at the expense of Indians in Natal. The estimated costs of the buildings eventually erected was for £20 000-00. It had a Principal, a Vice-Principal and a staff of six graduates from India.

1931

Teacher training began at Sastri College.

1932

Six Indian graduate teachers, from Sastri College, returned to India and white teachers filled the vacancies. Natal born Indians, with post ? matriculation qualifications had also joined the staff. A system of certification was introducing T.3 (with Matriculation), T.4 and T.5 were open to teachers who had not reached Matriculation level.

1933

Of the 88 women teachers employed in Indian schools, only 46 were Indian, the remaining 42 being Coloured and White.

1935

A class was established to train women teachers at the Mitchell Crescent School. A Domestic Science Department was opened at the Mitchell Crescent School in Durban

Mandela: Message to India

18 June 1994

[*On the occasion of an India-South Africa Solidarity Meet to discuss the post-apartheid South African scene, organised by the Indian National Social Action Forum (New Delhi, June 11, 1994), Nelson Mandela sent a message in his capacity as the President of South Africa and another in his capacity as the President of the African National Congress. Here the excerpts from Mandela's messages which bring out the bonds of solidarity that bind our two countries.* Editor]

There has been a golden thread that has bound our peoples together for many, many decades - a thread woven during the long, arduous and bitter years of struggle against common enemies: racism, imperialism and colonialism.

South Africa's relations with India date back centuries, starting in the seventeenth century when Indians formed part of the first batch of slaves who were brought from the East. They came in larger numbers from 1860 onwards as indentured labourers and so-called "passenger Indians."

Today, the South African Indian community is a million-strong, and it forms a full part of South African society. Hand-in-hand with other peace-loving South Africans, they have played an outstanding role in the struggle for a non-racial, non-sexist and democratic South Africa.

The noble and epic Indian struggle for freedom served as an inspiration to millions the world over to fight for their own emancipation and human dignity.

Forty-seven years after your great achievement we too have overthrown the yoke of racial oppression and tyranny. We rejoiced with you on that splendid occasion when the British standard was lowered on August 15, 1947, from the ramparts of the Red Fort in Delhi. We held our breath and celebrated the hoisting of the Indian tri-colour to signify the beginning of the new era in Indian history - and the beginning of the end of colonialism and imperialism on a world scale.

We have no doubts too, that you celebrated with millions of our people the moment of our own liberation and the birth of a new South Africa free from the scourge of racial tyranny and oppression.

Today, as we savour the moment of victory and begin the daunting task of building a new life for our people we recall with pride and gratitude the sterling contribution India and its people made towards the attainment of that objective. We cannot, for instance, forget the consistent and principled role India played, before and after independence, to focus world public opinion on the evils of the apartheid system. India's unilateral decision to sever all links - economic, political, diplomatic, etc. - with the apartheid state in the forties as an expression of her abhorrence to racism served as a spur to our freedom movement.

Your championing of our cause at the United Nations and other world fora further helped to galvanise the international community on to the side of the oppressed, exploited, voiceless and voteless South Africans. India thus was, in many respects, a pioneer in the international anti-apartheid struggle.

May we take this opportunity to express our deep appreciation and thanks to the people, government and leaders of India for their contribution made to the cause of freedom and human dignity in South Africa?

We are certain that the bonds of friendship and solidarity forged over the years will continue to grow. And may the golden thread woven in the common struggles against injustice and oppression never be broken.

Indian People of South History in more detail

It is June 1893 – a young Indian lawyer enters the Durban Court (British Colony of Natal), dressed in a frock-coat and turban. The magistrate, spotting the exotically dressed stranger, orders him to remove his headdress. The young lawyer refuses, walks out of court and pens an eloquent letter to the local press, defending the wearing of a turban. Subsequently described by the press as an 'unwelcome visitor', it was to be only the beginning for the young lawyer of many confrontations with discrimination in South Africa.

Today that young lawyer is celebrated as one of the most influential people of the twentieth century. His name? Mohandas Karamchand Gandhi, later in life known as *Mahatma Gandhi*. The honorific *Mahatma* meaning 'great soul'.

Gandhi spent 21 years in South Africa fighting for justice for the Indian population. His struggles and victories in South Africa are analogous to the history of Indian South Africans as a whole. The modern Indian South African community is a vibrant and crucial part of the diverse South African social fabric, however its early history was filled with hardship and disenfranchisement.

For most contemporary historians, Indian South African history started with the first indentured labourers arriving from India in 1860. That is not strictly true; Indians in South Africa were amongst the earliest settlers in the country. In fact the first two slaves who arrived in the Cape of Good Hope came from Bengal in India.

A common misconception is that slaves brought to the Cape in the 17th and 18th centuries were mostly from Africa and Indonesia. Research by Frank R Bradlow and Margaret Cairns in *'The Early Cape Muslims'* indicated that almost 70% of the slaves at the Cape came from Asia and more than a third from India (including what is Bangladesh today). The majority of the Indian slaves originated in Bengal, the Malabar Coast (Bombay, Goa) and the Coromandel Coast. Over a period of almost 150 years, thousands of Indian slaves were brought to the Cape. To such an extent that by the early 18th century the number of slaves exceeded the number of white settlers. Most of the Indian slaves worked on farms and were often subjected to extreme cruelty. Slaves who ran away from the harsh conditions on farms were flogged, branded and sentenced to hard labour when caught.

Due to the fact that the slaves were distributed over a large area, they lost their identity over time and their descendants became part of the Cape Malay or 'Coloured' communities. There were also many instances of female Indian slaves, especially Bengali women, marrying European settlers. This was mainly due to the fact that the ratio of European men to women at the Cape was 4:1 in the 17th century. Another contributing factor to the racially mixed marriages was that the children of slave couples were born into slavery, while the children of a slave married to a European were born free. Thus the progeny of Indian slave women eventually contributed to the greater Afrikaner gene pool. J. A. Heese, in *'The Origin of the Afrikaners 1657-1867'* concluded that in 1807, between 7 and 11 percent of the ancestors of the Afrikaner population were of African and Asian stock. Even ex-president F.W. De Klerk has been candid about his Bengali ancestry.

Indians also played an important role in the spread of Islam in South Africa: the first mosque in Cape Town was established in the early 19th century by Imam Frans and Imam Achmat, both from Bengal.

After slavery was abolished by the British parliament in 1833 there was a dearth of labour to develop the British Empire's rapidly expanding colonies. In order to fill the demand, indentured labourers from India were transported to British overseas colonies under five and ten year indenture contracts, with the option to return to India or exchange their free passage for a piece of land. Due to harsh taxation policies, industrialisation and a repressive administration, India was in the midst of a socio-economic crisis. The resulting massive levels of unemployment caused many peasants to look for a way out of their desperate circumstances.

In Southern Africa it was the British Colony of Natal that was most in need of cheap labour, especially on its sugar plantations. The local Zulu population refused to work for the colonists, so a deal was struck between the Natal colony, Britain and the British Indian government to import indentured labourers from India. The sugar magnates, like Sir James Liege Hulett, were instrumental in getting the agreement approved. (Today Tongaat Hulett Sugar is a multi-billion-dollar corporation.)

The first group of 342 arrived in Durban in 1860 from Madras (now called Chennai) in the Indian state of Tamil Nadu. Between 1860 and 1911 more than 150,000 Indian migrants were transported to Natal as indentured labourers. Most of them came from Tamil Nadu and Andhra Pradesh, with some from Uttar Pradesh and Bihar. They were a heterogeneous group: 90% were Hindus, the rest mostly Muslim with small numbers of Christians as well as a few Jains and Buddhists.

Although the majority worked on the sugar cane plantations, many also worked on the railways, dockyards, in the municipal services, in coal-mines and in domestic service. Their labour made an almost immediate contribution to the growth of the Natal Colony's economy. A fact that was widely acknowledged.

Conditions on the sugar plantations were often very harsh. Leading some commentators to label the indenture system as a new form of slavery. Workers were housed in barracks, isolated from the rest of the colony, with floggings, poor living conditions, separation from family members, and seven day work weeks the order of the day. This caused many of the first few groups to return to India. Their complaints of ill treatment made the Indian government halt the shipment of indentured labour to Natal. Recruitment resumed after a Commission of Enquiry lead to the promulgation of new regulations. In response to severe criticism, the British Imperial Legislative Council abolished the indenture system in 1916.

A second smaller group of Indian immigrants came to South Africa after 1860. Known as 'Passenger Indians' they were mainly Muslim and Gujerati-speaking Hindu traders, hawkers and merchants who had paid their own fares. About 1000 came to South Africa to take advantage of the commercial opportunities created by the burgeoning Indian community in Natal and the discovery of gold on the Witwatersrand.

The huge growth in the Indian population sparked intense anti-Asian sentiments amongst white colonists, who perceived Indian competition in agriculture and commerce as a threat. In fact only 10% were traders, the rest were ordinary labourers. Repeated demands for Indian immigration to cease and for Indians already in South Africa to be repatriated persisted until the 1960s. In 1961, Indians were finally officially recognised as a permanent part of the South African population.

A series of legal restrictions and discriminatory laws were implemented against the nascent Indian community:
- In 1891 the Statute Law of the Orange Free State prohibited Indians from owning businesses or farms in the Orange Free State. All Indian businesses were forced to close and the owners were deported from the Orange Free State without compensation.

- Act 17 of 1895, of the colony of Natal imposed a £3 tax on ex-indentured Indians, who failed to re-indenture or return to India after completion of their labour contracts. (£3 was equivalent to about 6 months' earnings)

- The Transvaal's Onerous Act 3 of 1885 barred Indians from owning land and confined them to locations.

- The Franchise Act of 1896, disenfranchised all Indians in Natal.

- The Asiatic Law Amendment Bill (The Black Act) of 1907, proposed the registration and fingerprinting of Indians, who would be required to carry registration certificates (similar to passes) at all times.

- The Transvaal Immigration Restriction Act of 1908 barred all non-resident Indians from entering the Transvaal without permits,

- The Immigrants Regulation Act, No 22 of 1913, classified all Asiatic persons as undesirable. It effectively put an end to Indian immigration and restricted Indian entry into provinces not of their domicile.

- A judgement by Justice Malcolm Searle in March 1913 in the Cape division of the Supreme Court rendered all marriages conducted according to Hindu or Muslim rites invalid. This meant that all married Indian women in South Africa were reduced to the status of concubines whilst their progeny were classified illegitimate and deprived of all their rights of inheritance, property, assets and legal claims.

After the National Party came to power in 1948, a further multitude of restrictive and discriminatory legislation was enacted under the apartheid system of racial segregation. Among the most notorious was the Group Areas Act which assigned racial groups to different residential and business sections in urban areas. Between the late 1950s and late 1980s more than 41,000 Indian families (about 278,000 individuals) were forced to leave Durban city and its suburbs, declared white areas under the Group Areas Act, and moved to peri-urban Indian settlements, the largest being Chatsworth and Phoenix, 30km north and south of Durban.

The Indian struggle for civil rights before 1948:

The Natal Indian Congress was founded by Gandhi and others in 1894 to fight discrimination against Indians. This followed by him setting up the Transvaal British Indian Association (forerunner of the Transvaal Indian Congress) in 1904. Gandhi also became editor of the newspaper, *Indian Opinion*, established in 1903 as the organ of the Natal and the Transvaal Indian Congresses.

In 1906, at a meeting of 3000 people in Johannesburg, gathered in protest against discriminatory laws, Gandhi introduced his Satyagraha (Sanskrit for 'truth and firmness') philosophy of passive resistance. It essentially meant non-cooperative, non-violent action and sacrifice.

The ensuing Satyagraha campaign lasted seven years and thousands of Indians were jailed, flogged, or shot for striking, refusing to register, for burning their registration cards or engaging in other forms of non-violent resistance. Strong international reaction to the repression of peaceful protesters forced the the Prime Minister, General Smuts, to negotiate with Gandhi. The resulting agreement led to the Indian Relief Act of 1914, which repealed the poll-tax and validated Indian marriages. However restrictions on land ownership, trading rights, immigration and movement between provinces remained unresolved and resistance would continue for many decades to come. In 1914 Gandhi left South Africa to begin his work in India.

The South African Indian Congress (SAIC) was founded in 1923 to form a national bulwark of resistance against growing segregationist tendencies in local and national legislation.

In 1945, Dr Yusuf Dadoo took over the leadership of the Congress in the Transvaal and Dr G.M. Naicker became the leader in Natal. They started following a policy of uniting Indian political organisations with other black bodies in order to present a common front. The Xuma-Naicker-Dadoo Pact of 1947, signed between the leaders of the two Indian Congress movements and the African National Congress (ANC) signalled a new era of solidarity between Africans and Indians in the struggle against discriminatory and oppressive laws.

Political involvement after 1948:

Passive Resistance Campaign 1946 – 1948:

The Asiatic Land Tenure and Indian Representation Bill of 1946 severely restricted the rights of Indians to own or occupy land. It also provided for the election of European representatives for Indian voters. The SA Indian Congress organised a march of 6000 people in Durban who occupied municipal land for several days. Many were arrested. As a result of international condemnation South Africa was refused the right to annex South-West Africa at the United Nations.

The Defiance Campaign, 1952:

The first large-scale, multi-racial political mobilisation against apartheid laws under the leadership of the ANC and the SAIC. A campaign commitment was made to mass action, boycotts, strikes and civil disobedience. 8,500 people including Nelson Mandela were arrested. Subsequent rioting lead to many being shot and killed. As a result harsh new measures for civil disobedience in the form of the the Public Safety Act and the Criminal Laws Amendment Act were introduced. On the positive side the publicity drew international attention and helped to cement solidarity against apartheid across racial lines.

The Congress of the People, June 1955:
The Congress Alliance was formed in 1953 as a broad non-racial front against apartheid policies. It consisted of the African National Congress, the South African Indian Congress, the Coloured People's Congress, and the Congress of Democrats, which housed radical and liberal white supporters.

It was decided that the alliance should convene a congress of the people, at which a freedom charter for a democratic South Africa would be adopted. The Congress of the People was eventually held at Kliptown, near Johannesburg, on 26 June, 1955.

The Freedom Charter, 1955:
The Freedom Charter affirmed that South Africa belonged to all its people, both black and white. It called for the scrapping of all forms of racial discrimination, the institution of a democratic system of

government, and equal protection for all before the law. The charter demanded equal access to education, social security, and employment. It also asserted a need for a fairer distribution of wealth through the nationalisation of industry, mines, banks, and the redistribution of land.

1956 Treason Trial:

Several prominent Indian leaders were arrested and accused of treason after their participation in the compilation of the Freedom Charter, which was seen as a communist manifesto by the government. Among them were Dr Yusuf Dadoo, leader of the SAIC and Dr Monty Naicker, leader of the Natal Indian Congress. The trial lasted till 1961 when the last of the accused were found not guilty.

Umkhonto we Sizwe, translated as "Spear of the Nation," was the armed wing of the African National Congress during its struggle against the apartheid regime.

Notable Indian members were Mac Maharaj, Billy Nair and Rashid Aboobaker Ismail.

During the 60s, 70s and 80s several Indian activists were banned from public speaking, arrested or forced into exile because they were members of banned organisations or planned/carried out sabotage attacks.

The Rivonia Trial took place between 1963 and 1964. Ten leaders of the African National Congress were tried for 221 acts of sabotage designed to overthrow the apartheid system. Two Indians were in the group of accused: Ahmed Kathrada and Billy Nair. Both were incarcerated on Robben Island with Nelson Mandela.

The Tricameral Parliament:

The South African government established a tricameral structure for the country's parliament in 1983, to give limited political power to the country's Coloured and Indian populations. The Indian 'House of Delegates' had power over so-called 'own affairs' that included education, social welfare, housing, local government, arts, culture and recreation. This limited form of democracy was opposed and derided from inside parliament by the official opposition and on the outside by the United Democratic Front, a huge coalition of anti-apartheid organisations. As a consequence, voter turnout in the two elections of its existence (1984 and 1989) was extremely low, with the elected officials having little credibility amongst the Indian electorate.

First democratically elected parliament, 1994:

There were 32 Indian South African members of the National Assembly (8% of the 400 seats), while the 1994 cabinet contained 4 ministers of Indian descent: Jay Naidoo, Mac Maharaj, Valli Moosa and

Kader Asmal. The first female speaker of the National Assembly, Frene Ginwala, was of Parsi-Indian extraction.

Indian South Africans today – the fast facts:

- ➢ 2,5% of the population.

- ➢ 1.3 million souls.

- ➢ 550,000 practised the Hindu faith according to the 2001 census. The balance mostly Muslim or Christian.

- ➢ The world's 7th largest Indian community outside India, and the biggest in Africa.

- ➢ The largest group of Indian descent born outside India in the world, i.e. born in South Africa and not migrant, compared to countries like the United States.

- ➢ Durban has more overseas Indians than any other city outside India.

- ➢ English is the first language of most Indian South Africans. A minority, especially the elders, still speak some Indian languages, such as Hindi, Tamil, Telugu, Urdu, Punjabi, and Gujarati as first language.

- ➢ The Tamil community has promoted a revival in the use of the Tamil language, and created increased language awareness.

- ➢ Average household income for Indian families is the second highest in the country after whites at ZAR251,541. (2011 Census)

The Legacy of the Indian South Africans:

South Africa has had as big an impact on the Indian community as they had on the country themselves. The epiphany for Gandhi's Satyagraha philosophy occurred when he was confronted by the convoluted and tortured realities of South Africa. A complex learning school that stood him well when he went on to agitate for the liberation of India from British colonialism.

Vice versa, his approach of non-violent, non-cooperative passive resistance set a template for decades of civil mobilisation against the apartheid structures. That lesson would not have been learned by the broader South African community if it was not for the support that he received from the local Indian community. A lesson that probably prevented much more blood from being spilled during the struggle for democracy.

The same challenges that confronted Gandhi upon his arrival in South Africa also confronted all other Indian immigrants. The fact that common obstacles to a better life were in all Indian migrants' way, meant that caste, religious and linguistic differences became less pronounced than in the mother country. It made for a more cohesive and integrated community.

On the political front many Indian South Africans made huge sacrifices and contributions in the fight against apartheid, on a scale vastly disproportionate to the size of their community. A civic role that continues today in various national and international, governmental and non-governmental roles.

From poor indentured sugar cane plantation workers to doctors, lawyers, economists, accountants, actors, directors of companies, writers, artists, ministers of cabinet and much more, they have shown grit and a true passion for their adopted country.

Other accomplishments:

The University of Durban-Westville (now part of the University of KwaZulu-Natal) was built with a rand-for-rand contribution from Indian South Africans and the government in the 1970s.

Food! Indian cuisine has been part of the South African culinary fabric for so long that many have probably forgotten that some of their favourite dishes and snacks were originally introduced by their Indian compatriots: samoosas, rotis, biryani and curry stews. Probably the most idiosyncratic would be 'bunny chow' – a hollowed out loaf of bread filled with curry, that originated in the Durban Indian community. It was a portable way for migrant workers to carry food to the sugar plantations. The apparent origin of the name is that 'bunny' is a corruption of 'bania', from the mostly Gujarati traders who started selling it. They were merchants who traditionally sold their wares under the 'bania' tree (also known as the banyan, or Ficus bengalensis) and were therefore called 'ban'.

A short list of Indian South Africans who have excelled in their respective fields:

Dr. Imtiaz Sooliman – founded the Gift of the Givers Foundation, the largest disaster relief group of African origin.

Pravin Gordhan – South African Minister of Finance.

Ebrahim Patel – South African Minister of Economic Development.

Fatima Meer – a South African writer, academic and screenwriter, known for her anti-apartheid activism.

Hashim Amla – first player of Indian descent to play Test Cricket for South Africa.

Navanethem Pillay – United Nation's High Commissioner for human rights.

Anant Singh – Academy Award nominated film producer

At a meeting of the YMCA in Johannesburg in 1908 Gandhi described his vision for the future of South Africa:

Indian Opinion' newspaper

History of the 'Indian Opinion' newspaper

On 4 June 1903 a very tired but fired up young man worked till 3am in the morning in the central business district of Durban. He then walked to his home in Sydenham as the last tramcar had long departed. On 5 June again he worked till 11pm - there was an urgency with which he worked. His goal was to get a new newspaper before the public. The first issue of Indian Opinion was dated 4 June but it was only on 6 June that it could be released. The young man was relieved but he could not relax. He had the next issue to think about and it was due in five days time. He wrote `I am now anxious about the second number. With a small staff, and lack of materials - types, etc., and facilities, we have to keep the paper up to the mark!'

This man was M.H. Nazar, a secretary of the Natal Indian Congress. His letters for this early period indicate that there were two other key individuals involved in the production of this new journal. Madanjit

Viyavaharik, the owner of the International Printing Press and Mohandas Gandhi, the Johannesburg lawyer. Nazar and Madanjit saw to the practicalities of producing the newspaper - this was no mean task for the paper was to be produced in four languages - English, Hindi, Gujerati and Tamil.

The translation of the articles was difficult as individuals proficient in two languages were required. Nazar would report 'The translators are not particularly clever, and they will not work at day time'. Some translations were simply 'shocking'. Then there was a shortage of types. Virji Damodar Mehta (who would one day found his own printing press, Universal Printing Press) asked Nazar not to use too many of the Gujerati letter 'a'. The editor himself did not know Tamil and had to explain the spirit of articles to translators whose English was not too good. Madanjit in the meanwhile had been running around getting the licence, advertisers and subscribers. The first issue which was some two months in the planning was finally out.

I start deliberately with Nazar, the first editor, and Madanjit the actual owner, to illustrate the point that there were many dedicated workers who made Indian Opinion a possibility. It was Nazar, in fact, who would set a high standard for those who would succeed him in the editor's chair. There was no question of taking money for his work, it was all for a `cause`. However there is no doubt that the main figure in the production of the paper was the thirty-four year old lawyer whose office was based in Rissik Street in Johannesburg. Nazar would suggest various lead articles but lest Gandhi should not understand he clarified the position. He expected these to be written by Gandhi. Over the years, Gandhi would direct the policy of Indian Opinion from Johannesburg, write articles, give direction and above all divert his earnings from his prospering practice to help sustain the paper. And over the years there were many dedicated workers and editors.

My task this evening is to explain what is the significance of this journal which by its second year had 887 subscribers. Over its entire 58 years existence its subscribers averaged at about 2000. The highest number in any one year was 3500. Compare this with the Guardian which in the 1930s began with a circulation of 1000 but grew rapidly over the years to top 50 000 by the mid-1940s. When Indian Opinion was reaching its dying days in 1961, the Guardian now published as New Age had a circulation of 20 000. The significance of Indian Opinion lies not in its size (which may be explained only partly in terms of the size of the Indian population) but in its content.

Indian Opinion was also not the first Indian newspaper in Natal. It had been preceded by a short-lived Indian World in 1898 and in May 1901

P.S Aiyar a Tamil journalist began a Tamil-English weekly Colonial Indian News. Aiyar's ventures reflected the precariousness of such undertakings as this too lasted for just a few years. Africans in colonial Natal had also been publishing newspapers for some time. There had been Inkanyiso yase Natal, Ipepa lo Hlanga and in April 1903 John Dube began his Ilanga lase Natal. In the eastern Cape where black journalism had an even longer history there was *Imvo Zabantsundu* run by John Tengo Jabavu and the more radical paper Izwi Labantu published by Walter Rubusana and Alan Soga from East London. Indian Opinion was launched at a time when just after the South African War all blacks felt disappointed with British rule and were concerned about the failure of the new order to bring about improvements in their political, social and economic status. The years after the war were marked by a proliferation of papers. Sol Plaatje . one of our most talented elites of the time began a Tswana-English weekly that served the northern Cape and Free State. Later, in 1909, in Cape Town Dr Abduraham would start the APO. These were just a few of the many papers emerging. The important point I would like to make is that Gandhi belongs to this generation of rising black journalists and editors who were all committed to improving the position of black people especially at a time when whites were moving towards forming a Union of South Africa within which blacks had such limited rights.

Indian Opinion marked Gandhi's apprenticeship as a journalist. In India he would go on to publishing many other journals, Young India, Navajivan, Harijan and his experience with Indian Opinion would prove crucial.

Indian Opinion began its life by adopting a very moderate tone. The editor proclaimed `we have unfailing faith in British justice'. It was by `well-sustained continuous and temperate constitutional effort that Indians would seek redress'. That is how the paper began and in colonial Natal there was reason to be cautious. The owners of Ipepa lo Hlanga chose to close down after it offended the Natal government with an article urging people Vukani Bantu! Rise Up you people'. For the time being Gandhi was anxious not to offend white officialdom but to secure their support to improve the position of Indians. The pages of Indian Opinion provide a valuable historical record of the disabilities that Indians suffered under. It also provides an invaluable record of the life of the political life of the Indian community. It represents an alternate voice to that of newspapers such as the Natal Mercury which were often hostile to Indian interests. Soon Gandhi would move from political petitioning to active resistance and his paper changed too.

One significant moment in the paper's history came in 1904 when Gandhi relocated it to a one hundred acre farm named Phoenix just 24 kms from Durban. This reflected the influence of Leo Tolstoy and John Ruskin on Gandhi. Gandhi drew on Tolstoy's distaste for city life, his praise of agricultural labour and his renunciation of wealth. From Ruskin he drew the idea that all labour whether that of the professional or the manual labourer was equal but also that 'the life of a tiller of the soil and the handicraftsman, is the life worth living.' At Phoenix the press workers were governed by a new work ethic - they would all have a share in the land, in the profits if there were any, they would grow crops to sustain themselves and they would work jointly to produce Indian Opinion. Thus the history of Indian Opinion becomes intertwined with Phoenix, Gandhi's first communal settlement. While at Phoenix the rhythm of life was dictated by the production of the paper, in India it was the spinning wheel which was the centre of ashram activity.

Indian Opinion played a very significant role in the early years of the twentieth century by fostering the idea of one united Indian community and a national identity. This was no mean task for Indians were divided by religion, caste, class, and even Indian regional affiliations. 'we are not, and ought not to be, Tamils or Calcutta men, Mohammedans or Hindus, Brahmins or Banyas, but simply and solely British Indians'. Indian Opinion especially highlighted the poor conditions under which indentured labourers worked. Editorials asked

'Is all well on the Estates', cases of harsh treatment by employers were publicised and the astoundingly high rate of suicide was pointed out. A campaign to end the system was launched and editor Henry Polak, a friend of Gandhi's went to India to mobilise support. Indian Opinion was a means of bringing news about Indians in the colonies before the public in India.

Indian Opinion and political activism on the part of its editors became an established tradition. This is what would, throughout the 20th century distinguish Indian Opinion from other newspapers that would arrive on the scene during the 20th century. All but one of its editors spent some time in jail. This tradition began during the satyagraha campaign between 1906 and 1913 which began because of attempts to impose passes on Indians in the Transvaal. The newspaper came into its own. In 1904 its aims had simply been to educate whites in South Africa about Indian needs and wants.

From 1906 onwards it became a vehicle for challenging state laws and urging defiance of these when these were clearly unjust. It is this that elevates this tiny newspaper produced from a farm to one of world significance for it became linked with Gandhi's transformation to a mass movement leader and his philosophy of satyagraha which can be interpreted as active non-violent resistance. The law was translated into Gujerati, readers were urged to defy the law, from Johannesburg Gandhi wrote a regular Johannesburg Letter explaining to anxious Indians what steps they should take and what the reaction of the authorities would be.

Inspirational stories of resistance were published such as the life of Socrates who chose death rather than bow to the Athenian officials. The paper played a fundamental role on defeating the registration drive of officials. Its pages paid tribute to local resisters and Brian Gabriel, one of Natal's earliest Indian photographers, provided visual coverage. Gandhi who by 1909 had spent 177 days in jail - and there would be more to come - extolled the virtues of prison life, a life of poverty, and urged readers not to pursue wealth at a time when there was higher moral calling.

According to Gandhi `Satyagraha would have been impossible without Indian Opinion'. Gandhi recalled `the paper generally reached Johannesburg on Sunday morning. I know of many, whose first occupation after they received the paper would be to read the Gujerati section through from beginning to end. One of the company would read it, and the rest would surround him and listen. ' So as we acknowledge the importance of satyagraha as a weapon that evolved on South African soil, that inspired many anti-colonial, anti-imperial, anti-apartheid movements and movements in a quest for justice, a weapon that would ultimately bring the mighty British Empire to its heels in India, so we should acknowledge Indian Opinion. It was a key mobilising device. Gandhi also had a bigger campaign in mind - he had his eyes on India and in the pages of Indian Opinion he published his book Hind Swaraj which set out his vision for an independent India. Indian Opinion faced its first banning order - these issues were prohibited in India.

Although Indian Opinion began by advocating Indian rights it also focussed on the disabilities of other blacks in South Africa - the devastating provisions of the Land Act of 1913, the pass struggles of Africans were publicised and African achievements too were celebrated. In the 1950s especially under the editorship of Manilal Gandhi, Gandhi's second son, the newspaper became more focussed on human rights rather than the rights of Indians only. It became a central medium for disseminating the meaning of satyagraha and of propagating Gandhism. In a significant move in 1957 the English section of IO was renamed Opinion. In the words of Sushila Gandhi who took on the editorship after Manilal's death, the name change was to reflect the "Oneness of Man", the belief in `a new sense of nationhood & transcends cultural and racial barriers and holds before all the ideal of a unified nation whose various people shall be bound together by their love of their country and their belief in the ideals on which their freedom should be founded. Gandhi she asserted belonged to not just "India and Indians only & the greatest teachers of humanity do not belong to their tribes or national groups they belong to humanity'. And this is what we commemorate today that great belief in fundamental human rights and the constant striving and vigilance to ensure its attainment.

Gandhi left behind a tough legacy for his successors at Indian Opinion to follow. This was not a commercial undertaking, it was a paper for political, social and moral education. It would be very remiss of me to not pay tribute to those who helped Gandhi shape his legacy in those early years and those who continued that legacy for several decades thereafter. There were the trustees of Phoenix Settlement and all those who on a regular basis who saved Indian Opinion from its dire financial straits. These names would be too numerous to mention. We need to recognise though in a roll call of honour at least the family of Parsee Rustomjee.

There were many editors - Nazar, Hebert Kitchin, Henry Polak, Albert West, Manilal Gandhi who was the paper's longest serving editor for 36 years and Sushila Gandhi. There were many contributors, assistants and acting editors too - Gandhi's nephews, Chhaganlal and Maganlal

Gandhi, Lewis Walter Ritch, Albert Christopher, Pragji Desai, Surendra Medh, Shantilal Gandhi, P.R. Pather, Jordan Ngubane, Christopher Gell, Homer Jack, Arun Gandhi, Sita Gandhi-Dhupelia, Ranjith Nowbath , Pat Poovalingam and Natoo Babenia. When Indian Opinion published its last issue on 4 August 1961, Alpha Ngcobo had served for 41 years after coming to the press as a young man of twenty years. Perumalsamy Rajoo served for 27 years, D. Gangabissoon sixteen , S. Ramdhar and R. Baijnath thirteen years each. They made up the small staff that daily gathered in the International Printing Press.

Sushila Gandhi above all ended a 34 year old link with the paper. She had come as a young bride of 20 years in 1927 and began in the press by composing types - each letter had to be handset - for over 58 years advances in printing technology were deliberately avoided. Time stood still and manual labour was favoured over machines. Sushila soon progressed to writing and editing the Gujerati sections and then took over after her husband's death. A photograph shows a lone woman in the printing press working amongst the handful of men. Indian Opinion provided a place where women could work as equals and be freed of cultural and traditional restraints and that was Gandhi's doing and teaching. And that too is what we celebrate and commemorate today. I thank you.

End of the Book

###

Thank you for reading my book. If you enjoyed it, won't you please take a moment to
leave me a review at your favorite retailer?

Thanks!

Sampson Jeremiah

www.ingramcontent.com/pod-product-compliance
Lightning Source LLC
Chambersburg PA
CBHW031103080526
44587CB00011B/802